Pearson Education Limited

Edinburgh Gate, Harlow,

Essex CM20 2JE, England

and Associated Companies throughout the world.

ISBN 0 582 46136 7

First published in Great Britain by Hutchinson 1968

This edition first published 2001

Original copyright © Arthur C. Clarke and Polaris Productions Inc 1968

Text copyright © Penguin Books 2001

3 5 7 9 10 8 6 4 2

Typeset by Pantek Arts Ltd, Maidstone, Kent

Set in 11/14pt Bembo

Printed in Spain by Mateu Cromo, S.A. Pinto (Madrid)

Published by Pearson Education Limited in association with

Penguin Books Ltd, both companies being subsidiaries of Pearson Plc

For a complete list of the titles available in the Penguin Readers series please write to your local
Pearson Education office or to: Marketing Department, Penguin Longman Publishing,
80 Strand, London, WC2R 0RL

Contents

Introduction

'In fact it's about three million years old. You are looking at the first proof of intelligent life beyond the Earth.'

The speaker is Dr Roy Michaels, Chief Scientist at the Clavius Base on the Moon. The audience has been carefully chosen, because it is too soon to tell the world's population that they are not alone in the universe. On the screen behind Dr Michaels is a photograph of a black object about three metres high, of regular shape and with straight edges. It was certainly made by an intelligent form of life, and it was found buried under the surface of the Moon.

If it is a message from another time, from a distant star, why has it been put there? A possible answer comes soon afterwards, when the first light of the sun touches the object. It then sends out a powerful radio signal, aimed exactly at Saturn. As one of the scientists says, 'You hide a sun-powered object in darkness – only if you want to know when it is brought out into the light.' So, far out in space, there may be intelligent beings who now know that men and women have taken their first steps away from Earth.

This book is a journey. We watch as people move forward from their early beginnings into the future, and as one man, on the space ship *Discovery*, travels a billion kilometres from Earth to make contact again among the rings of Saturn.

In 1964, before men had even landed on the Moon, the film director Stanley Kubrick was looking for a story for a science fiction film. He asked Arthur C. Clarke for help, and the two men worked together on the development of the plot. Clarke wrote the novel (which came out in 1968), while Kubrick made the film, and both became extremely famous.

PART ONE Ancient Night

Chapter 1 The Road to Death

Very little rain had fallen for a long time, for at least ten million years. Here, in the place that one day would be called Africa, the man-apes of the grasslands were fighting a battle to stay alive, and they were not winning.

About fifty of them lived in caves on the side of a small dry valley. There was a stream running down the middle. If the weather was very hot, its water dried up and the man-apes were thirsty.

When the first light of morning came into the cave, Moon-Watcher saw that his father had died in the night. He did not know that the Old One was his father, because he did not know what a father was. But he felt a little anxious as he dragged the dead body out of the cave. Outside, he did something that no other animal in the world could do – he stood up.

Moon-Watcher was bigger than the others in his group. He was nearly a metre and a half high, though very thin because of the constant hunger. His hairy body was half-way between ape and man, but his head looked quite human. His forehead was low, but there were signs of intelligence in his eyes.

As he walked down the slope, the rest of the group saw him and began to come out of their caves. They moved towards the stream for their morning drink. Moon-Watcher walked on until he found a small bush. He left the body there, knowing that animals would do the rest. He never thought of his father again.

His two females, the adults from the other cave, and most of the young ones were looking for berries among the small trees further up the valley. Only the babies and the very old were left in the caves. If there was any extra food at the end of the day, they might be fed. If not, they would stay hungry.

Moon-Watcher climbed the slope to join the group. After some time he found honey in a dead tree. This did not happen very often, and the group was happy. Of course, they also collected a number of bee stings, but they hardly noticed these. Now, although Moon-Watcher was still hungry, he was not actually weak with hunger. He could not expect more than that.

He led his group back to the stream. The Others were there, as usual. There were about thirty of them, and they looked exactly the same as Moon-Watcher's own group. As they saw him coming, they began to dance, shake their arms and shout, and his people did the same.

And that was all that happened. Although the man-apes sometimes fought among themselves, they could do little harm to each other. Their teeth were not sharp and their bodies were protected by thick hair. Also, they did not often have enough energy for fighting. After a time, the man-apes on both sides grew quiet and began to drink the muddy water.

On the grassland near the caves there were many animals, but the man-apes knew of no way to kill one of them. In fact, they could not even imagine the idea of killing one. In the middle of so much food, they were slowly dying of hunger.

That night a cold wind blew. Moon-Watcher hardly moved when the screams came from one of the lower caves. He knew what was happening before he heard the sound of the leopard. But Moon-Watcher did not think of going to help. He lay quietly, as all the others did.

Later, he went outside and sat on a rock. He looked up and down the valley, then at the Moon. The man-apes were the only animal that ever did this. Moon-Watcher had done it since his childhood. He was old now, twenty-five years old. If he was lucky, he might live another ten years.

He stayed on the rock for some time, sleeping and waking but always listening. If any animal moved in the area, Moon-Watcher would know about it. But he did not see the bright light, brighter than any star, that crossed the sky twice, rising high and sinking down to the east.

Chapter 2   The New Rock

Late that night Moon-Watcher suddenly woke up. He sat up in the darkness of the cave, looking out into the night, and fear entered his soul. He had never heard a sound like this in his life. The big cats approached in silence, except perhaps for the occasional breaking of a stick or a fall of earth. But this was a continuous crashing noise that grew steadily louder. Even the elephants did not make as much noise as this.

Then he heard a sound which he could not understand, because it had never been heard before in the history of the world. It was the sound of metal hitting stone.

◆

Moon-Watcher saw the New Rock when he led the group down to the river in the first light of morning. He had almost forgotten his fear during the night, and did not connect this strange thing with it.

It was three times his height, but when he reached out his hands to each side, it was not as wide. When he walked round and looked at it from the side, it was quite thin. And he could see right through it. In fact, he only knew it was there when the sunlight flashed on its edges. He put out his hand and touched its cold surface.

It was a rock, of course, and it had grown during the night. He knew of small round plants that grew during the night and looked a little like rocks. These tasted good, so Moon-Watcher put out his tongue and tasted the new rock. A few seconds were enough to make him understand that this thing was not food. So he continued on his way to the river and soon forgot all about it.

In the last light of day, as the group climbed back towards the caves, the sound began. It was low and continuous. It came from the new rock, and they all stopped to listen. Then they turned and, like sleep-walkers, began to move towards the rock. They sat in a circle round the strange thing as the darkness came down and a light grew inside it.

The noise grew louder and lights began to flash and move, making patterns that changed all the time. The man-apes watched, their mouths open, not knowing that the thing was examining their minds.

Suddenly one of them stood up. He picked up a piece of grass and tried to tie it into a knot. His eyes were wide with terror as he struggled to make his fingers do what they had never done before. He failed. The broken pieces of grass fell to the ground and he froze into stillness again.

Another man-ape began to move. This one was younger and after some time it succeeded. On the planet Earth the first knot had been tied.

Others did stranger things. Some held their hands out and tried to touch their fingertips together. Some were made to stare at patterns in the rock, watching lines which became thinner and thinner until they could not be seen.

Moon-Watcher stood and picked up a stone. Now on the new rock was a series of circles, each one smaller than the next. The smallest one was black inside. Obeying the instructions in his brain, he threw the stone. He had never done this before, and he missed by some distance.

Try again, said the command. He found another stone and threw. It hit the edge of the rock and made a ringing sound. His third throw hit the circles, only centimetres from the central black one. A strong feeling of pleasure passed through his body.

One by one, every member of the group was tested and then allowed to feel either pleasure or pain. Then the light in the rock died away. Shaking their heads, the man-apes got up and began to walk along the path that led to their caves. They did not look back at the strange light that was showing them the way to their homes – and to an unknown future, perhaps even to the stars.

Chapter 3   Education

In the morning Moon-Watcher and his group had no memories of what had happened the night before. When they went out to find food, they hardly looked at the new rock as they passed it. They could not eat it and it could not eat them, so it was not important.

But that night the noise from the new rock started again, and once again the group went to sit around it. This time it seemed only interested in a few of the man-apes, and one of them was Moon-Watcher. Once again he felt the thing exploring his mind, and then he began to see things. He saw a group of man-apes resting near the entrance to a cave. The male, female and two young ones were obviously eating well. They were quite fat and their hair was shiny. He put his hand on his own thin body and thought about the difference between himself and the picture in his mind.

Later, as he sat outside the cave, Moon-Watcher felt the beginnings of a new emotion. For the first time, he felt unhappy with his life and he wanted to change it. He had taken one small step towards being human.

Night after night the rock showed him the four man-apes who were eating so well, and this made him feel even more hungry. The rock was helping this feeling to grow, because it was changing the patterns in his brain. If he lived, these changes would be passed on to his children.

It was slow work, but the rock was patient. If it failed, there were other similar rocks doing the same thing across half of the world. A hundred failures would not matter if one success could change history.

◆

As the line of wild pigs crossed the path, Moon-Watcher stopped suddenly. Pigs and man-apes had always ignored each other, because they did not compete for the same food.

But now Moon-Watcher stood looking at them. Something was happening in his mind which he did not understand. He started to search the ground. He did not know what he was looking for, but he would know it when he found it.

It was a heavy pointed stone about fifteen centimetres long. As he swung his hand round, puzzled by the increased weight, he felt a new sense of power. He started to move towards the nearest pig.

It was a young and foolish animal, and it felt no fear until much too late. It went on looking for food in the grass until Moon-Watcher's hammer ended its life. The other pigs continued to feed, because the murder had been quick and silent.

The man-apes gathered round. One of them picked up the wet stone and began to hit the dead pig. Others helped with sticks and stones until the pig was a broken mess.

Then they became bored. Some walked away, others stood around the body, and the future of the world waited on their decision. It was quite a long time before one of the young mothers began to taste the stone she was holding.

And it was even longer before Moon-Watcher, despite all he had been shown, really understood that he need never be hungry again.

Chapter 4   The Leopard

The tools they had been programmed to use were simple enough. There was the hand-held stone and the long bone. With these they could kill, but they needed something else, because their teeth and fingers could not pull apart any animal larger than a rabbit. Luckily, Nature had provided the perfect tool. It was simply the lower jaw-bone of an animal, with the teeth still in place. There would be no great improvement on this until the invention of steel.

With these tools in their hands, they could feed on the limitless food of the grasslands and become the masters of the world. They accepted their new life easily, and did not connect it with the rock that was still standing beside the path to the river.

However, the group still had occasional days when they failed to kill anything. At the end of one of these, coming back to the caves empty-handed, they found a wild cow lying by the path. Its front leg was broken, but it still had plenty of fight left in it. Moon-Watcher's group circled the animal carefully, then moved in and killed it with their long bones and stones.

This took some time, and now it was getting dark. Moon-Watcher knew it would be dangerous to stay any longer. Then he had a wonderful idea. He thought hard, and in time managed to imagine the cow – *in the safety of his own cave*. He took its head and began to drag it along the path. The others understood and helped him.

The slope was steep and the animal was heavy, but eventually they got it inside the cave. As the last of the light left the sky, they started to eat.

Hours later, his stomach full, Moon-Watcher suddenly woke up. At first he did not know why, but then, from a long way away, he heard the sound of a falling stone. Afraid but curious, he moved to the entrance of the cave and looked down the slope.

Then he was so afraid that it was long seconds before he could move. Only six metres below, two shining golden eyes were staring straight up at him. He was frozen with fear and hardly saw the powerful body behind them, moving silently from rock to rock. The leopard had never climbed so high before. It had ignored the lower caves and followed the smell of blood up the hillside.

Seconds later, the night became noisy as the other man-apes cried out in fear. The leopard made an angry sound but it did not stop. It reached the entrance and rested for a moment. The smell of blood was all around. Then it came silently into the cave.

And here it made its first mistake, because as it moved out of the moonlight, even its night-hunter's eyes were at a disadvantage. The man-apes could see it against the moonlight outside, but it could not see them.

The leopard knew that something was wrong when the first bone hit the side of its head. It swung its front leg and heard a scream of pain as the leg struck soft flesh. Then something sharp went into its side – once, twice, and a third time. It turned round to strike at the shadows dancing on all sides.

Something hard hit it across the nose. Its teeth closed on a white object, but it was only dead bone. And now something was pulling its tail. It turned around, throwing its attacker against the wall of the cave. But whatever it did, it could not escape the bones and stones that were hitting it from all sides. The noises it made turned from pain to fear and then to terror. The hunter was now the hunted, and it was trying to escape.

And then it made its second mistake, because in its fear it had forgotten where it was. It ran straight out of the entrance at high speed – too high for the steep slope. It rolled and turned and cried as it fell. There was a heavy sound as it crashed into some rocks far below.

Moon-Watcher stood at the entrance to the cave. He listened to the silence as the last stones stopped falling. Then he started to shout and dance, because he knew that his whole world had changed. A long time later, he went back into the cave and, for the first time in his life, he had an unbroken night's sleep.

Chapter 5 Meeting at Dawn

As he led the group down to the river in the early morning, Moon-Watcher paused uncertainly in a familiar place. The new rock had left as mysteriously as it had appeared. Moon-Watcher tried to remember what had been there, but could not. He put the problem from his mind, and it never entered his thoughts again.

◆

From their side of the stream, the Others saw Moon-Watcher and a dozen other males moving against the dawn sky. At once they began to shout and threaten in the usual way, but this time there was no answer.

Steadily and silently, Moon-Watcher's group walked down the hill above the river, and as they approached, the Others went quiet. Their pretended anger died away, and was replaced by real fear. They saw the long bones and knives, but these did not alarm them because they did not understand their purpose. But they knew that the group was moving in a new and different way.

For a moment Moon-Watcher stopped at the water's edge. Then he raised his arms high, showing what had been hidden by the hairy bodies of his companions. He was holding a thick branch, and on the end of it was the head of the leopard. The mouth had been fixed open with a stick, and the great teeth shone white in the first light of the rising sun.

Most of the Others were frozen with fear, but some began to move back. Still holding the bloody head up high, Moon-Watcher started to cross the stream, and the rest of his group followed him.

When Moon-Watcher reached the far side, the leader of the Others was still standing in place. Moon-Watcher swung the branch down on his head, and the leopard killed one more time.

Screaming with fear, the Others ran away in all directions. Moon-Watcher stood looking at the dead leader. Now he was master of the world, and he was not quite sure what to do next.

But he would think of something.

Chapter 6   The Beginning of Man

There was a new animal on the planet, spreading slowly out from the African grasslands. There were still very few of them, and there was no reason to believe that they would continue to live, where so many bigger animals had failed.

In the hundred thousand years since Moon-Watcher had lived and died, the man-apes had invented nothing. But they had started to change. Their great teeth were becoming smaller, because they were not so necessary now. The sharp-edged stones that could be used to dig out roots, or cut through flesh, had begun to replace them. This meant that the man-apes could still eat when their teeth became damaged or old, and so they lived longer. And as their teeth grew smaller, their jaws became shorter. The greater variety of sounds they made were not speech, but speech was now possible.

And then the world began to change. Four Ice Ages came and went, with two hundred thousand years between each of them. They killed much of the planet's early life, including many man-apes. But those tool-makers who continued to live had been remade by their own tools.

From using bones and stones, their hands had learned new skills. And these allowed them to make better tools, which had developed their hands and brains even more. The process of change became faster and faster, and the result was Man. And somewhere in that long period of time they had learned to speak. Now knowledge could be passed from parent to child, so each new age could profit from the ones that had gone before.

Unlike the animals, who knew only the present, Man had discovered a past, and was beginning to look towards a future.

He was also learning to use the forces of nature. When he discovered fire, he began the long process of technical change. In time, stone would be replaced by iron, and hunting would change to farming. The group would become a village, and the village would grow into a town.

And as his body became more and more defenceless, his power to attack became more frightening. With stone and iron he had discovered many ways to kill, and quite early he learned how to kill from a distance. From throwing sticks and stones to dropping bombs, his power increased until it was great enough to destroy the planet.

If he had not had those weapons, Man would never have become master of the world. For ages they had served him well.

But now, as long as they existed, he was living on borrowed time.

PART TWO   TMA-1

Chapter 7   Special Flight

Dr Heywood Floyd had left Earth many times before, but as the moment of take-off approached, he still felt nervous.

The jet that had rushed him here from Washington, after that midnight meeting with the President, was now dropping down towards one of the most exciting parts of the world. Here, along thirty kilometres of the Florida coast, were the greatest structures of the Space Age. Near the horizon he could see the shining silver tower of the last Saturn 5, a museum now for twenty years. Not far away from it stood the great building where all the early ships had been built.

But these things now belonged to the past, and he was flying towards the future. As his plane turned, he could see the spaceplane in a pool of light, being prepared for its flight to the stars. It seemed very small from this distance, until he looked at the tiny figures all around it. Then he remembered that it was more than sixty metres across the narrow 'V' of its wings. And they were preparing this enormous machine just for him.

Though it was two o'clock in the morning, a crowd of reporters and cameramen were waiting for him when he stepped off the plane. But he could say nothing except 'no comment' as he walked through them.

The stewardess greeted him as he entered the spaceplane.

'Good morning, Dr Floyd. I'm Miss Simmons. I'd like to welcome you on board.'

He looked at the twenty empty seats. On her advice, he chose the front one on the left, because it would offer the best view. He sat down, put on the safety belt and fixed his bag to the next seat. A moment later, the loudspeaker came on.

'Good morning,' Miss Simmons said. 'This is Special Flight 3 to Space Station 1.'

It seemed she wanted to follow the normal routine, and Dr Floyd smiled.

'Our flight time will be fifty-five minutes, and we will be weightless for thirty minutes. Please do not leave your seat until the safety light is lit.'

Floyd looked over his shoulder and called, 'Thank you.' She smiled, a little embarrassed.

He leaned back in his seat and relaxed as the Captain's voice came through the loudspeaker.

'Take off in fifteen seconds. You will be more comfortable if you start breathing deeply.'

As the great machine left the ground, he felt himself sinking deeper and deeper into his seat. It was difficult to move, but there was no real discomfort. In fact the blood rushing round his body made him feel young again, and he wanted to sing aloud. This was certainly possible, because no one could hear him above the great noise of the engines.

His mood changed quickly as he realized he was leaving Earth and everything he had ever loved. Down there were his three children, motherless since his wife had died in a plane crash ten years ago.

The pressure and the noise both suddenly decreased, and he heard the Captain's voice again.

'Preparing to separate from lower stage. Here we go.'

There was a slight movement as the spaceplane freed itself from its carrier. The lower stage would fly the sixteen thousand kilometres back to Florida, and it would then be prepared to lift another spaceplane away from the Earth.

When the spaceplane's own engines started, the speed increased only a little. In fact he felt no more than normal gravity. But it was impossible to walk, since 'up' was straight towards the front of the plane. If he had been foolish enough to leave his seat, he would have fallen right to the back.

It was an uncomfortable feeling, as if his seat was fixed to a wall, with all the others below him. He was trying to ignore it when dawn suddenly exploded outside.

In seconds they moved through layers of red and pink and gold and blue into the shining white light of day. Though the windows were heavily coloured to reduce the light, Floyd was still half-blinded for several minutes. He was in space, but he could not see the stars.

Then he felt his weight decreasing as the spaceplane levelled.

The engines slowed down and then fell silent, and they were in orbit. If he had not worn a safety belt, Floyd would have floated out of his seat; his stomach felt as if it wanted to do so anyway. He hoped that the pills he had been given half an hour and fifteen thousand kilometres ago would do their work. He had been spacesick just once in his career, and that was too often.

The pilot's voice came through the loudspeaker. 'Please observe all zero gravity rules. We will be arriving at Space Station 1 in forty-five minutes.'

The stewardess came walking up the narrow passage to the right of the seats. Her feet came off the carpet slowly, as if they were stuck in glue. In fact she was walking on the bright band of magnetic carpeting that ran the full length of the floor – and of the ceiling. The bottoms of her shoes were also magnetic.

'Would you like some coffee or tea, Dr Floyd?' she asked cheerfully.

'No, thank you,' he smiled. The plastic drinking tubes always made him feel like a baby.

Miss Simmons stayed as he opened his bag.

'Dr Floyd, may I ask you a question?'

'Certainly,' he answered, looking up over his glasses.

'My boyfriend works at Tycho,' she said, 'and I haven't heard from him for over a week. Is it really true about illness on the Moon?'

'If it is, there's no need to worry. Remember the illness in 1998? A lot of people were sick, but no one died. And that's really all I can say.'

She smiled pleasantly and straightened up.

'Well, thank you anyway, Doctor. I'm sorry to take up your time.'

'No problem at all,' he said, then opened his bag and began to look through his endless technical reports. There would be no time for reading when he got to the Moon.

Chapter 8 Space Station 1

Half an hour later the pilot announced, 'We make contact in ten minutes. Please check your safety belt.'

Floyd put away his papers. The last 500 kilometres involved a lot of movement from side to side as the spaceplane tried to get into position. It was best to sit back and relax.

A few minutes later he had his first sight of Space Station 1, 300 metres across and turning slowly. Behind it was Earth. From his height of 320 kilometres, he could see much of Africa and the Atlantic Ocean.

The central part of the Space Station was now coming towards them. Unlike the rest of the structure, it was not turning. In this way, a spaceship could land on it without being spun round.

Floyd felt the spaceplane make contact. A few seconds later, the airlock door opened and a man entered.

'Pleased to meet you, Dr Floyd. I'm Nick Miller, Station Police. I'll look after you till the moonship leaves.'

They shook hands, then Floyd smiled at the stewardess and said: 'Please give my thanks to the rest of the crew. Perhaps I'll see you on the way home.'

Very cautiously − it was more than a year since he had been weightless, and it would be some time before he got used to it − he pulled himself hand over hand through the airlock and into the large circular room at the centre of the Space Station. The walls, floor and ceiling were covered with soft material, and there were handholds here and there. Floyd held on to one of these firmly, while the whole room started to turn until its speed was the same as the Space Station.

As it went faster, he was gently pushed back, and now, instead of standing against a circular wall, Floyd was lying on a curved floor. He stood up. The force of the spin had created artificial gravity. It was weak here, but would increase as he moved away from the centre.

From the central room he followed Miller down curving stairs. At first he felt so light that he almost had to force himself downwards. He did not gain enough weight to move almost normally until he reached the passenger lounge, on the outside edge of the great turning circle.

'Can I get you anything while we're waiting?' Miller said. 'We leave in about thirty minutes.'

'I'd like a cup of black coffee – two sugars.'

'Right, Doctor – I'll get it.'

Miller walked away, and Floyd turned to look around the lounge. There were very few people there, but one of them was walking straight towards him.

'Hello, Dimitri,' he said, because there was no escape.

Dr Dimitri Moisewitch shook hands energetically. He was a scientist from the USSR. He was also one of Floyd's best friends, and for that reason he was the last person Floyd wished to talk to here and now.

Chapter 9   Moon Ship

'Hello, Heywood,' the Russian said, shaking hands. 'Nice to see you again. How are you – and the children?'

'We're fine,' Floyd said. 'We often talk about the wonderful time you gave us last summer.' He was sorry he could not sound more sincere; they really had enjoyed the holiday at Dimitri's house in Odessa.

'And you – I suppose you're on your way up?' Dimitri asked.

'Er, yes – my flight leaves in half an hour,' answered Floyd. 'Do you know Mr Miller?'

The policeman had now approached, and was standing at a respectful distance holding a plastic cup of coffee.

'Of course. But *please* put that down, Mr Miller. This is Dr Floyd's last chance to have a proper drink – let's not waste it. No – I mean it.'

They followed Dimitri out of the main lounge into a smaller room with large windows. Soon they were sitting at a table, watching the stars move past. Space Station 1 turned round once every minute, producing an artificial gravity equal to the Moon's. This gave passengers on their way to the Moon a chance to get used to what they would experience there.

'Now,' said the Russian, putting down his drink, 'what's all this about illness at the US Base? I wanted to go there on this trip, but they wouldn't let me. What's happening? Do you want any help from our medical services?'

'I'm sorry, Dimitri – we've been asked not to say anything at the moment. Thanks for the offer, though.'

'Hmmm,' said Dimitri. 'Seems odd to me that you, a scientist, should be sent up to the Moon to look at an illness. Do you have much medical experience?'

Floyd smiled. 'I suppose I'm the sort of scientist that knows about lots of different subjects. Maybe that's why they chose me.'

'Then do you know what TMA-1 means?'

Miller's head came up in surprise, but Floyd stayed calm. 'TMA-1? What an odd expression. Where did you hear it?' he asked.

'Never mind,' answered the Russian. 'You can't fool me. But if you've found something you can't handle, don't leave it until too late before you shout for help.'

Miller looked at his watch.

'We're due to board in five minutes, Dr Floyd,' he said. 'I think we'd better move.'

Though he knew that they still had twenty minutes, Floyd got up quickly. Too quickly, because he had forgotten the one-sixth of gravity. He had to reach for the table to keep himself down.

'Goodbye, Dimitri,' he said. 'It was nice seeing you.' It was not true, this time, but he felt he had to say it.

As they left the room, Floyd said, 'Phew, that was difficult. Thanks for rescuing me.'

'You know, Doctor,' said Miller, 'I hope he isn't right about us running into something we can't handle.'

'*That*,' Floyd answered, 'is what I intend to find out.'

Forty-five minutes later, the Aries-1B moonship pulled away from the station. There was none of the power and noise of a take-off from Earth, just a quiet whistling as the three engines started up. The gentle push lasted no more than fifteen minutes, and during that time it was quite possible to get up and walk around.

Floyd had the whole ship to himself again, though it had been designed for thirty passengers. It was strange and rather lonely, but he had the undivided attention of a steward and stewardess, as well as two pilots and two engineers. He doubted that any man in history had ever received such service, and it was unlikely that anyone would do so in the future. He should try to enjoy this trip, and the pleasure of weightlessness. With the loss of gravity he had — at least for a while — lost most of his worries. Someone had once said that you could be frightened in space, but you could not be worried there. It was perfectly true.

The steward and stewardess, it seemed, were keen to make him eat for the whole twenty-five hours of the trip, and he had to wave away many unwanted meals. It was not difficult to eat in zero gravity, despite the fears of early astronauts. The plates were fixed to the table, and all the food was made sticky. Hot soup was not possible, but apart from this the menus were fairly normal.

Drinks, of course, were a different matter; all liquids had to be kept in plastic squeeze-tubes.

When he was not eating, Floyd gave some attention to the official reports he had brought with him. When he got tired of these, he connected his page-sized news screen to the ship's information system and read the latest reports from Earth. One by one he could look at the world's electronic newspapers. Each of the stories on the front page had a number. When one was chosen, the little square grew until it filled the screen.

There was just one sleep-period, when the main lights were switched off. Floyd lay down on the sofa and got his arms and legs inside the fixed sheet that would prevent him moving away into space. When he woke up, the Moon was filling half the sky. He moved through to the Control Room to watch the final stages of the approach.

The ship was just above the line dividing night and day. It moved towards the dark side, and he could see the sharp tops of the mountains lit by the reflected light from Earth. He felt some weight return as the ship slowed down. Now they were above an enormous crater with a flashing light in its centre. A voice was calling above the whistle of the jets.

'Clavius Control to Special 14, you are coming in nicely. Please make all control checks now.'

The pilot pressed some switches, green lights flashed, and he called back, 'Control checks completed. All OK.'

Now the mountain tops were high above the ship, and then Floyd lost sight of them as the engines blew up clouds of dust. He felt the plane touch the ground, and the pilot shut down the engines. It took Floyd some minutes to accept that they had arrived, and some time longer to believe that after a completely normal flight he had landed on the Moon.

Chapter 10   Clavius Base

Clavius, two hundred and forty kilometres across, is the second largest crater that can be seen from Earth. Here, Man was building his first permanent base on the Moon. In an emergency, it could produce everything it needed to support life. Solid chemicals and gases could be produced by processing local rocks. In a great hothouse, under lamps at night and sunlight by day, thousands of small plants grew to provide oxygen and food. The scientists could turn these, and other material grown in water, into very good copies of bread and meat and vegetables.

The hundreds of men and women who worked on the Base were all highly-trained scientists and technicians, carefully chosen before they had left Earth. Though living on the Moon was physically easier than in the early days, it was still psychologically difficult. It did have its attractions, though. One of them was the low gravity, which produced a general feeling of happiness. However, this had its dangers. It was simple enough to travel in a straight line. The problem came when you tried to turn a corner, because your body continued in the same direction. It took time, and a few small accidents, for newcomers to get used to this, and more experienced Base workers tried to stay away from them until they had.

◆

The mountains that had seemed so large just before landing had mysteriously disappeared, hidden below the Moon's steeply curving horizon. Around the ship was a flat grey area, brightly lit by earthlight.

A number of service vehicles were now rolling up to the Aries-1B, moving on enormous tyres. But Floyd was watching a small bus that was bringing the people who wanted to meet him.

There were a number of bangs as it connected to the ship, then the sound of air moving as pressure was equalized. The inside door of the airlock opened, and the welcoming party arrived.

It was led by Ralph Halvorsen, the Base Commander. With him was his Chief Scientist, Dr Roy Michaels, and a group of scientists and managers. They seemed happy to see him, ready to unload some of their worries.

'Very pleased to have you with us, Dr Floyd,' said Halvorsen. 'Did you have a good trip?'

'Excellent,' Floyd answered. 'No problems, and the crew looked after me very well.'

The conversation continued as the bus moved away from the ship and into an entrance passage. A large door opened, then closed behind them. This happened again, and a third time. When the last door had closed, they were back in atmosphere again. The people Floyd saw were wearing normal clothes.

After a short walk they arrived in an office area. Floyd was happy to be surrounded by computers and telephones again after his time in space.

Halvorsen led Floyd towards a door labelled *BASE COMMANDER*, but before he could show him inside his office, there was an interruption. The door opened, and a small figure ran out.

'Daddy! You've been outside! And you promised to take me!'

'Well, Diana,' said Halvorsen, 'I only said I'd take you if I could. But I've been very busy meeting Dr Floyd. Shake hands with him — he's just come from Earth.'

The little girl — Floyd decided that she was about eight — held out a hand. Her face was slightly familiar. Then, with a shock, he understood why.

'I don't believe it!' he said. 'When I was here last, she was just a baby!'

'She had her fourth birthday last week,' Halvorsen answered proudly. 'Children grow fast in low gravity. But they don't age so quickly – they'll live longer than we do.'

Floyd stared at the confident little lady, noting that she was thinner as well as taller than an Earth child. 'It's nice to meet you again, Diana,' he said. Then sudden curiosity made him ask, 'Would you like to go to Earth?'

Her eyes widened in surprise, then she shook her head,

'It's a nasty place – you hurt yourself when you fall down. And there are too many people.'

So here, Floyd told himself, is one of the first of the Spaceborn. There would be more of them in the future. The time was fast approaching when Earth, like all mothers, would say goodbye to her children.

Halvorsen managed to persuade his daughter to leave him in peace, and the two men went into the office. It was only five metres square, but it had the same furniture as a Base Commander's office on Earth. There were signed photographs of important politicians – including one of the President of the United States – on one wall, and pictures of famous astronauts on another.

Floyd sat back in a comfortable leather chair and accepted a glass of wine, made in the Base laboratory.

'How's it going, Ralph?' he said. The wine was quite good.

'Not too bad,' Halvorsen said. 'However, there is one thing you should know before you meet the others. My people are angry because they can't communicate with Earth. They think their families will be worried that they've died of this "illness".'

'I'm sorry about that,' said Floyd, 'but no one could think of a better story, and it's worked. I met Moisewitch at the Space Station, and even he believed it.'

'Well, that should make the police happy.'

'Not too happy – he'd heard of TMA-1. He didn't know

what it was, but the name has got out. We need to find out what the thing is, and quickly.'

Chapter 11   Anomaly

Halvorsen led Floyd into a room that could hold a hundred people easily. With a white screen on the end wall, and its rows of seats, it looked like a conference centre. However, the notices and pictures on the walls showed that it was also the centre of local cultural life.

About forty or fifty people were waiting for Floyd, and everyone stood up politely as he entered. Floyd sat down in the front row, while the Commander stood up on the platform and looked around his audience.

'Ladies and gentlemen,' Halvorsen began, 'I needn't tell you that this is a very important occasion. We are delighted to have Dr Heywood Floyd with us. He has just completed a special flight from Earth to be here.'

Some of the audience clapped. Floyd stood up for a moment, said a word of thanks and sat down again.

'Dr Michaels,' said Halvorsen, and walked back to his seat.

The Chief Scientist stood up and moved to the platform. As he did so, the lights were turned off and a photograph of the Moon appeared on the screen. At its centre was the white ring of a large crater.

'Tycho,' said Michaels, although everybody there knew its name. 'During the last year we have been checking the magnetism of the whole region. This was completed last month, and this is the result that started all the trouble.'

Another picture flashed on the screen. It was a map with many lines going across it. Generally, these were spaced quite far apart, but in one corner they came close together and formed a series of smaller and smaller circles. It was quite obvious that there was something strange here. In large letters across the bottom of the map were the words: *TYCHO MAGNETIC ANOMALY – ONE (TMA-1)*. Stamped on the top right of the map was another word: *SECRET*.

'At first we thought it was just a large magnetic rock, but this would be very unusual for the area. So we decided to have a look.

'There was nothing on the surface, just the usual flat ground under a thin layer of moon-dust. So we started to dig, and we dug for two weeks – with the result you know.'

The darkened room became suddenly quiet as the picture on the screen changed. Though everyone had seen it many times, they all leaned forwards, hoping to find new details. On Earth and Moon, less than a hundred people had been allowed to see this photograph.

It showed a man in a bright yellow spacesuit, standing at the bottom of a large hole, and holding a stick marked off in tenths of a metre. Next to him was a piece of black material, standing about three metres high and a metre and a half wide.

'TMA-1,' Dr Michaels said, quietly. 'It looks new, doesn't it? However, we've now been able to date it positively, from what we know of the local rocks.

'In fact it's about three million years old. You are looking at the first proof of intelligent life beyond the Earth.'

Chapter 12   Journey by Earthlight

The travelling laboratory was now moving across a flat area at 80 kilometres an hour. It was a large vehicle, carried on eight wheels. But it was much more than this; it was also a base in which twenty men could live and work for several weeks.

As he looked ahead out of the window, Floyd could see a marked way stretching ahead of them, where dozens of vehicles had flattened down the soft surface of the Moon. At regular distances apart there were tall thin poles, each carrying a flashing light. No one could possibly get lost on the three-hundred kilometre journey from Clavius Base to TMA-1, although it was still night and the Sun would not rise for several hours.

The stars overhead were only a little brighter than on a clear night on Earth, but there was one thing that destroyed the idea of being there. This was Earth itself, bright and round, hanging above the northern horizon. It shone down with a light much stronger than the light of the full Moon, making this a land of blue and green.

As he sat with Halvorsen and Michaels in the front observation lounge, immediately beneath the driver's position, Floyd's thoughts turned again and again to the black object and its age of three million years. As a scientist, he was used to thinking about much longer periods of time, but these had been in connection with the movements of stars and the slow changes of the universe. Mind, or intelligence, had not been involved.

Three million years ! All of written history, with its countries and its kings, its successes and disasters, covered only about a thousandth of this great period of time. Man himself, and most of the animals now alive on Earth, did not even exist when the black puzzle was so carefully buried there.

Dr Michaels was sure it had been buried, and not by accident. When they dug down, they found that it was sitting on a wide platform of the same black material. Whoever put it there wanted it to stay in the same place for a long time.

And so the old question had been answered. Here was proof, beyond all doubt, that there was other intelligent life in the universe. But with that knowledge came sadness. The unknown visitors had missed humans by a long period of time.

And where did they come from, these creatures who could cross space while Man was still living in trees? The Moon itself? No, that was completely impossible. If there had ever been life here, it had been destroyed during the last period when the craters were formed, when the surface was white-hot.

Earth? Very unlikely, though perhaps not quite impossible. If intelligent non-human creatures had lived on Earth, they would have left many other signs of their existence. But nothing else had been found before TMA-1 was discovered on the Moon.

That left two possibilities – the planets, and the stars. But all scientific opinion was against intelligent life anywhere else in the Solar System* – or life of any kind except on Earth and Mars.

So perhaps these visitors had come from the stars – but that was even more difficult to believe. The journey from Earth to the Moon seemed quite long, but the nearest star was a hundred million times more distant ...

Floyd shook his head because he knew he was wasting his time. He must wait until there was more knowledge.

'Please check your safety belts,' said the loudspeaker suddenly. 'Forty degree slope approaching.'

Floyd had just put his belt on again when the vehicle slowly moved over the edge of a slope as steep as the roof of a house. The earthlight, coming from behind them, was now very faint, and the vehicle's own front lights had been switched on. They were going down the side of Tycho, and three hundred metres below the slope levelled out into a great flat area.

'There they are,' Michaels said, but Floyd had already noticed the group of red and green lights several kilometres ahead. Soon he could see, shining in the earthlight, a group of temporary buildings for the workers living there. Near these were a radio tower, a group of parked vehicles and a large pile of broken rock.

*Solar System: the Sun and its planets, including Earth.

'You can just see the crater,' said Michaels. 'Over there on the right – about a hundred metres from the tower.'

So this is it, thought Floyd, as the bus rolled past the buildings and came to the edge of the crater. He leaned forwards for a better view as the vehicle moved slowly down the slope. And there, exactly as he had seen it in the photographs, was TMA-1.

Floyd stared, shook his head and stared again. Even in the bright earthlight, it was hard to see the thing clearly. His first impression was a flat object that seemed to have no thickness at all. This was because, although he was looking at a solid body, it reflected so little light that he could only see its shape.

The bus stopped about six metres from it. Then the lights were switched on all around the crater. Where light touched the object, it seemed to be swallowed up by the black surface.

A box of tricks, thought Floyd, with a sudden feeling of fear – waiting to be opened by curious Man. And what will he find inside?

Chapter 13   The Slow Dawn

The main building was only six metres square, and it was now very overcrowded. In this double-walled space, six scientists and technicians lived, worked and slept.

Floyd and Dr Michaels each put on a spacesuit and walked into the airlock. As the noise of the pumps died away, Floyd felt himself move into silence. The sound of his suit radio was a welcome interruption.

'Pressure OK, Dr Floyd?' said Michaels. 'Are you breathing normally?'

'Yes, I'm fine.'

The outside door opened and, walking slowly, Floyd followed Michaels through the lock. He looked around and, without warning, the tip of the radio tower above his head seemed to catch fire as the rising Sun touched it.

They waited while the Base Commander and two of his assistants came through the airlock, then walked slowly towards the crater. It was still in shadow, but the lights all around lit it up brightly. As Floyd walked down the slope, he felt a sense of helplessness. Here, at the gate of the Earth, was a mystery that might never be solved.

His thoughts were interrupted by his suit radio.

'Base Commander speaking. Could you all form a line? We'd like to take a few photos. Dr Floyd, will you stand in the middle – Dr Michaels – thank you . . .'

Though it seemed funny at first, Floyd had to admit that he was glad somebody had brought a camera. It would be a historic photo, and he hoped his face could be seen through the helmet of his suit.

'Thanks, gentlemen,' said the photographer. 'We'll ask the technical staff at the Base to send you copies.'

Then Floyd turned his full attention to the black object – walking slowly round it, examining it from every side. He did not expect to find anything, because he knew that every square centimetre had already been looked at very closely.

Suddenly the Sun lifted itself over the edge of the crater and shone on the flat side of the object. But the object seemed to take in all of the light and reflect nothing. Floyd decided to try a simple experiment. He stood between the object and the Sun, and looked for his own shadow on the smooth black sheet. There was nothing to be seen. He thought of the amount of heat that was falling on that surface; if there was anything inside, it would be rapidly cooking.

For a moment he wondered about energy from the Sun. But who would be crazy enough to bury a sun-powered object six metres underground?

Floyd looked up at the Earth. Only a few of the six billion people there knew of this discovery. How would the world react to the news when it was finally broadcast?

In fact every person of real intelligence would find his life, his values, his ideas, changed a little. Even if nothing was ever discovered about TMA-1, Man would know that he was not alone in the Universe.

Floyd was still thinking about this when his helmet speaker suddenly gave out a high electronic scream. While he was trying to find the sound control, four more of the screams struck his ears. Then there was silence.

All around the crater, figures were standing in shocked surprise. So there is nothing wrong with my equipment, Floyd told himself; everyone heard those sounds.

After three million years of darkness, TMA-1 had greeted dawn on the Moon.

Chapter 14   The Listeners

A hundred million kilometres beyond Mars, Deep Space Recorder 79 continued with its observations of radio noise and distant stars. Anything that it saw or heard was recorded in its memory and sent back to Earth every twenty-four hours. There, machines waited to examine the information, and then add it to the thousands of kilometres of tape stored in the World Space Centres in Washington, Moscow and Canberra.

And now Deep Space Recorder 79 had noted something strange – a faint but unmistakable movement across the Solar System, quite unlike anything it had noticed in the past. Automatically, it recorded the direction, the time and the strength.

Orbiter M15, circling Mars twice a day, and even Explorer 5, heading out into the cold emptiness beyond Pluto, also noted a peculiar burst of energy. They reported it automatically to the memory stores on Earth.

The computers were not programmed to notice the connection between the three sets of signals from machines millions of kilometres apart. But as soon as he looked at his morning report, the Chief Controller at Goddard knew that something strange had passed through the Solar System during the last twenty-four hours.

He had only part of its path, but when the computers had done their work, it was as clear as a line of footprints across snow. A pattern of energy had jumped from the face of the Moon and was heading out towards the stars.

PART THREE   Between Planets

Chapter 15   *Discovery*

The ship was still only thirty days from Earth, but sometimes David Bowman could hardly believe that he had ever really lived there. His life now was in the closed little world of *Discovery*. When he spoke to Frank Poole about this, he found that Frank had the same feelings. But this sense of separation was easy enough to understand. In the fifty years since men had first gone into space, there had never been a mission quite like this. *Discovery* was going past Mars and Jupiter, all the way to Saturn. And she would never return.

For *Discovery* it would be a one-way trip – but her crew had no intention of dying. If all went well, they would be back on Earth within seven years. For five of these years they would be in hibernation, while they waited for rescue by *Discovery II* – which had not yet been built.

It was a calculated risk, like all voyages into the unknown. But experiments had proved that human hibernation was perfectly safe, and it had opened up new possibilities in space travel.

The three other members of the crew, all scientists who would not be needed until the ship reached Saturn, would sleep through the whole flight there. In this way, a lot of food and other materials would be saved. Also, they would be fresh and rested after the ten-month voyage.

Then the ship would orbit Saturn, giving them a hundred days to map and study a world eighty times the area of Earth, and surrounded by fifteen known moons – one of them as large as the planet Mercury. They would radio their discoveries back to Earth, so even if the explorers never returned, these would not be lost.

Sometimes Bowman envied Whitehead, Kaminski and Hunter, his three unconscious colleagues. They were free from all problems and all responsibility. Until they reached Saturn, the outside world did not exist.

But that world was watching them while they slept. In the Control Room there were five small screens. The last two, marked *POOLE* and *BOWMAN*, were plain and lifeless. Their time would not come until a year from now. The others were covered with small green lights which showed that everything was well with the three sleepers. They also had a set of moving lines showing heartbeat, breathing and brain activity. This last line hardly moved at all. If any consciousness remained, it was beyond the reach of instruments.

Bowman knew this from personal experience. Before he was chosen for this mission, his reactions to hibernation had been tested. When all the instruments were in place on his body, he had seen a pattern of moving lights for a few seconds.

Then they had disappeared, and darkness had come. He never felt the drugs take effect, or the first touch of cold as his body temperature was reduced to a few degrees above freezing . . .

When he woke up, it seemed that he had hardly closed his eyes. But he knew that was wrong. Somehow he was sure that years had passed.

Had the mission been completed? Had they already reached Saturn, finished their work and gone into hibernation? Was *Discovery II* here to take them home?

He opened his eyes, but there was little to see. Warm air was blowing across him, and quiet music came from a speaker behind his head. It was slowly growing louder and louder . . .

Then a relaxed, friendly voice – he knew it came from a computer – spoke to him.

'Hello, Dave. Do not get up or attempt any violent movements. Do not try to speak.'

He did not want to get up. He was happy knowing that the rescue ship had come and that soon he would be seeing other human beings.

Some time later, another voice spoke to him. This time it was human. It was also familiar.

'Hello, Dave. You're fine. You can talk now. Do you know where you are?'

He thought about this, and had to admit to himself that he was not really sure. He shook his head.

'Don't worry, Dave. This is Frank Poole. Everything's fine. We're going to open the door now and pull you out.'

Soft lights came on, and then all his memories returned to him, and he knew exactly where he was.

Though he had come back from the furthest borders of sleep, and the nearest borders of death, he had been gone only a week. The mission was still more than a year in the future.

He was still in the crew trainer at the Houston Space Flight Center.

Chapter 16   Hal

But now Texas was a tiny spot, and even the United States was hard to see. Most of *Discovery*'s many telescopes were pointed at other planets, in the direction she was travelling. There was one, however, that looked back at Earth. It was fixed to the edge of the great dish that sent the ship's radio messages. It made sure that the dish pointed in the right direction. Messages could then come and go along a path that became more than three million kilometres longer every day.

At least once every watch period, Bowman went to the screen that showed the view from that telescope and looked back towards his home. Sometimes he saw a familiar shape, like the Pacific. And he remembered days and nights spent on its islands.

The sixth member of the crew cared for none of these things, as it was not human. It was the HAL 9000 computer, the brain and nervous system of the ship. In the 1980s, Minsky and Good had shown how it was possible to build a computer simply by designing a learning programme. In this way, an artificial brain could be grown in a very similar way to the growth of a human brain. The result was a machine that could do most things that a human brain could do, but with much greater speed and certainty.

Hal had been trained for this mission as thoroughly as his human colleagues, but in a much shorter time. His main job was to check, repeatedly, all the systems on the ship – oxygen pressure, temperature, conditions in the hibernators, and everything else that the crew depended on to stay alive.

The first computers had received commands through keyboards, and had replied through printers and screens. Hal could do this if necessary, but most of his communication was through the spoken word. Poole and Bowman could talk to Hal as they would to a human being; he replied in the perfect English learned during the short weeks of his electronic childhood.

The question of whether Hal could actually think had been answered by the British mathematician Alan Turing back in the 1940s. Turing had explained that if you had a long conversation with a machine, and you could not tell if it was a machine or a man, then the machine *was* thinking. Hal could easily pass the Turing test.

Chapter 17   Daily Life

Bowman and Poole each worked for twelve hours out of twenty-four, and they were never both asleep at the same time. The officer-on-duty normally remained in the Control Room, while his assistant did the general housekeeping, checked the ship or relaxed in his room.

Bowman's day began at 06.00 hours, when Hal woke him up. He did his exercises, then washed and shaved before eating his breakfast and reading that morning's *World Times*. On Earth, he never read the paper as carefully as he did now. Even the smallest pieces of news interested him as they flashed across the screen.

At 07.00 he took over from Poole in the Control Room, bringing him a plastic tube of coffee from the kitchen. If there was nothing to report and no action to be taken, he checked all the instrument readings, and did a series of tests designed to recognize possible problems. By 10.00 this was finished, and he started on a study period.

Bowman had been a student for more than half his life, and would continue to be one till he retired. At thirty-five, he had already taken in as much knowledge as two or three university educations would provide. He had never been able to stay interested in only one subject, and this made him very suitable for his present job. Poole was the same, and the two of them, with some help from Hal's enormous stores of information, could handle any problems that were likely to appear during the voyage.

At midday Bowman went to the kitchen and left the ship to Hal while he prepared his lunch. Poole joined him for this meal before leaving for his six-hour sleep period. Their menus had been planned with as much care as the rest of the mission. The food, most of it freeze-dried, was excellent and only needed to be put into the tiny automatic oven. They could enjoy what tasted like – and, equally important, *looked* like – orange juice, eggs (any style), steak, roast meats, fresh vegetables, various fruits, ice-cream, and even freshly-baked bread.

After lunch, from 13.00 to 16.00, Bowman made a slow and careful tour of the ship, or as much of it as could be visited. *Discovery* measured almost a hundred and twenty-five metres from end to end, but the crew spent most of their time inside a twelve-metre pressurized ball in the centre.

The central slice of this ball turned continuously, producing an artificial gravity equal to the gravity of the Moon. That was enough to allow for something like normal living.

Like all vehicles designed for deep space travel, *Discovery* had been put together in orbit above the Earth. The large numbers of instruments on the outside of her body would be destroyed by entry into an atmosphere, or even the pull of a planet's gravity. She was a creature of pure space – and she looked it.

At around 16.00, Bowman finished his inspection and made a detailed report to Mission Control. Then he listened to Earth, and sent back his reply to any questions. At 18.00 hours, Poole woke up and took command.

Bowman then had six off-duty hours, to use as he liked. Sometimes he continued his studies, or listened to music or watched films. Much of the time he wandered through the ship's enormous electronic library, following the voyages of earlier explorers. He travelled with Pytheas out of the Mediterranean, along the coast of a Europe that was just leaving the Stone Age; with Magellan round the world for the first time, or with Cook to the great unknown continent of Australia. And he began to read the *Odyssey*★ which spoke to him more than any other book across the great distance of time.

For relaxation he could always play various board games with Hal. If Hal really tried, he could win every time, but the crew would get too depressed. So he had been programmed to win only 50 per cent of the games, and his human partners pretended not to know this.

At 20.00 Bowman had dinner, again with Poole, and after this there was an hour during which he could make and receive personal calls from Earth.

Like all his colleagues, Bowman was unmarried; it was not fair to send family men on a mission of such length. Though many women had promised to wait until the crew's return, no one really believed this. At first, Bowman and Poole had been making personal calls to girls on Earth quite regularly, though they knew that many other ears must be listening. But in time, the warmth and the frequency of these conversations grew less. They had expected this. It was one of the problems of an astronaut's life.

★The *Odyssey*: an ancient story by the Greek poet Homer about Odysseus's long journey home from war.

However, in general the two men were fairly content with their routine lives. Their greatest hope was that nothing would spoil its peace and quiet in the weeks and months ahead.

Chapter 18   Through the Asteroids

Week after week passed, and *Discovery* moved beyond the orbit of Mars towards Jupiter. Ahead lay the most dangerous part of the journey, an area of space crossed by the orbit of more than a million known asteroids.

Only four of these were over a hundred kilometres across, but even the smallest could completely destroy the ship. However, the chances of this were very low. The average distance between asteroids was at least a million and a half kilometres.

On Day 86 they were due to make their closest approach to a known asteroid. It had no name – just the number 7794 – and it was a fifty-metre rock that had been discovered in 1997.

When Bowman came on duty, Hal reminded him of the meeting. The path of the asteroid against the stars was already on the screens. There was also the information that 7794 would miss them by only fifteen hundred kilometres, at a relative speed of a hundred and thirty thousand kilometres an hour.

When Bowman asked Hal for the telescopic view, a small number of stars flashed onto the screen. There were a number of points of light, but nothing that looked like an asteroid.

'Show me which one it is,' Bowman said, and immediately four lines appeared on the screen, surrounding a tiny spot of light. He stared at it for many minutes, wondering if Hal could be mistaken, then he saw that the spot was moving. It might still be half a million kilometres away, but its movement showed that it was much closer than anything else they could see.

When Poole joined him in the Control Room, six hours later, 7794 was much bigger and moving faster against its background. They both stared at it. Though they knew that 7794 was only a lifeless piece of rock, it was also the only solid thing they would see this side of Jupiter.

As it raced past them at over thirty-six kilometres a second, the automatic cameras took dozens of photographs, which would later be sent back to Earth.

Within an hour, 7794 was just a spot of light again. The next time Bowman came on watch, it had gone completely. They were alone again, and would remain alone until the first of Jupiter's moons came towards them, three months from now.

Chapter 19   Passing Jupiter

Even from thirty million kilometres away, Jupiter was already the biggest object in the sky ahead. The planet was now a pale pink circle, about half the size of the Moon when seen from the Earth. Moving around its middle were the bright stars of Io, Europa, Ganymede and Callista. Each one of them was as big as a planet, but here they were just satellites of an enormous master.

In fact, Bowman had not really understood how big Jupiter was until, one day in the electronic library, he saw a picture. It showed the surface of Earth taken off, then fixed like the skin of an animal on the shape of Jupiter. Against this background, all the continents and oceans of Earth appeared smaller than India on a map of the world.

When Bowman used the ship's telescope, he saw only racing clouds that had been pulled out into long bands by the planet's fast turning speed. Hidden beneath those clouds was more material than in all of the other planets of the Solar System. And what *else*, Bowman wondered, was also hidden there?

Over the radio connection with Earth, the information was going back in a constant stream. They were now so far from home that, even travelling at the speed of light, their signals were taking fifty minutes for their journey. Though the whole world was looking over their shoulders, watching through their eyes and their instruments as Jupiter approached, it would be almost an hour before the news of their discoveries reached home.

Discovery passed within thirty thousand kilometres of Europa, and all instruments were aimed at the approaching world. Here were twenty-two million square kilometres of land which, until this moment, had never been more than a tiny spot in the best telescope. From a distance it had seemed like an enormous snowball, and closer observation showed that it really was a brilliant white. Unlike the dusty Moon, its surface was covered with shining objects that looked like large pieces of ice. Almost certainly these were formed mainly from water that Jupiter's gravity had somehow failed to capture.

As quickly as it had rushed out of the sky ahead, Europa dropped behind the ship, and now Jupiter itself was only two hours away. Even though Hal constantly checked and rechecked the ship's orbit, it was difficult to believe they were not flying straight into the enormous planet.

Now was the time to drop the atmospheric probes which, it was hoped, would continue to operate long enough to send back some information from below the clouds. As they slowly fell away, it was possible to see that the ship was in a steady orbit and would circle the planet safely.

And now, for the first time, they were going to lose the Sun. Though it was much smaller now, it had been with them for the whole of their five-month journey. As their orbit dived into the shadow of Jupiter, they watched it sink into the great clouds. There was a moment of flashing fire all along the horizon, then night came.

But the great world below was not wholly dark. Faint rivers of light moved from horizon to horizon. Here and there they gathered into pools of liquid fire, always moving, constantly changed by what was happening below. It was a wonderful sight, and it held Poole and Bowman's attention.

'Earth signal is dying rapidly,' announced Hal. 'We are entering the first silent area.'

They had been expecting this, but they felt a great loneliness. The radio silence would only last for an hour, but that hour would be the longest of their lives.

Jupiter was now an enormous wall of fire, stretching out of sight above them – and the ship was climbing straight up the side of it. Though they knew they were moving far too quickly for even Jupiter's gravity to capture them, it was hard to believe that *Discovery* had not become a satellite of this enormous world.

At last, far ahead, there was light along the horizon. They were leaving the shadow, heading out towards the Sun. And then Hal announced, 'I am in radio contact with Earth. I am also happy to say that the orbit has been successful. Our time to Saturn is one hundred and sixty-seven days, five hours, eleven minutes.'

That was within a minute of the original calculation. *Discovery* had successfully used the enormous gravity of Jupiter to increase her own speed by several thousand kilometres an hour. She had drawn energy from the great planet itself, which was now carrying it deeper into space.

But the laws of nature remained unbroken. As the speed of the ship had increased, Jupiter had slowed down, but by such a small amount that it could never be measured. The time had not yet come when Man could leave his mark on the Solar System.

As the light grew quickly around them, and the small Sun lifted again into Jupiter's sky, Poole and Bowman reached out silently and shook each other's hands.

Though they could hardly believe it, the first part of the mission was safely over.

Chapter 20   The World of the Gods

But they had not yet finished with Jupiter. Far behind, the two probes that *Discovery* had sent out were making their first contact with the atmosphere.

One was never heard from again. It had probably entered too steeply and burned up before it could send any information. The second was more successful. It sliced through the upper layers of Jupiter's atmosphere, then swung out into space again. It had then lost so much speed that, as planned, it began to fall back again towards the planet. Two hours later, it re-entered the atmosphere on the daylight side – moving at over a hundred thousand kilometres an hour.

Immediately it was surrounded by a cloud of gas, and radio contact was lost. There were anxious moments of waiting then, for the two watchers in the Control Room. They could not be certain that the probe would not burn up completely.

But the protective cover did its job, long enough for the probe to slow down. It then pushed out its scientific instruments and began to look around. On *Discovery*, now almost half a million kilometres away, the radio started to bring the first news from Jupiter.

Most of it was details about pressure, temperature and a dozen other changing features which the scientists on Earth would study later. However, there was one message that could be understood; it was the TV picture.

At first they could only see yellow mist, mixed with red areas that moved past the camera at high speed as the probe fell at several hundred kilometres an hour. The mist grew thicker, and it was impossible to tell if the camera was seeing for ten centimetres or ten kilometres. Then, suddenly, the mist disappeared as the probe fell out of this first layer of cloud.

The scene below was so strange that for a moment it was almost meaningless to an eye accustomed to the colours and shapes of Earth. It looked like an endless sea of gold, with great waves running across it. But there was no movement, and it could not possibly be an ocean because the probe was still high in the planet's atmosphere. It had to be another layer of cloud.

Then the camera caught something. Many kilometres away, coming up through the cloud, was a curiously regular mountain. Around the top of this were other small white clouds, all about the same size, all quite separate.

Poole and Bowman stared at this, the first sight of something on Jupiter that might be solid. But they would learn nothing more, because now the probe was reaching the end of its life. As it sank lower and lower, the pressure of the gas on it grew greater. With one warning flash, the picture disappeared.

Poole and Bowman had the same thought in their minds. If there was life down there, how long would it take to find it? After that, how long before men could follow this first probe — and in what kind of ship?

PART FOUR   Edge of Darkness

Chapter 21   Birthday Party

The familiar sound of 'Happy Birthday' died away among the screens of the Control Room. The Poole family, standing round a birthday cake on Earth, went suddenly silent.

Then Frank's father said, 'Well, son — can't think of anything else to say at the moment, except that our thoughts are with you, and we're wishing you the happiest of birthdays.'

'Take care, darling,' Mrs Poole said, tearfully. 'God be with you.'

Then they all said goodbye, and the film ended. Poole continued to stare at the screen, thinking that all this had happened more than an hour ago. By now, his family had gone their separate ways. It only made him feel further away from home.

'Sorry to interrupt the celebrations,' said Hal, 'but we have a problem.'

'What is it?' Bowman and Poole both asked.

'I am having difficulty in staying in contact with Earth. The trouble is in the AE 35 unit. I believe it may fail within seventy-two hours.'

'We'll take care of it,' Bowman replied. 'Put Earth on the screen.'

They studied their home planet for some time. The picture was coming to them from the TV camera fixed to the edge of the big radio dish. Unless the narrow beam was pointing straight at Earth, they could neither send nor receive messages. At the moment, it seemed to be working perfectly.

'Hal, do you know what the trouble is?' asked Bowman.

'It comes and goes, and I can't tell exactly. But it does seem to be in the AE 35 unit.'

Bowman's first thought was to ask Hal for more details, but he decided to try himself. He ran his mind over the thousands of systems on the ship, and after a few moments the information came to him. The antenna was kept pointing at Earth by motors controlled from the central computer. But the instructions went to the AE 35 unit first, where they were changed into something that the motors could understand. It was like a nerve centre in the body, which translates the brain's signals into instructions for movement. Now Bowman had a question he could ask Hal.

'What do you suggest?' he said.

'The best idea is to replace the unit with a spare, so we can check it over.'

'Put it up on the screen,' Bowman said.

Bowman studied the drawing, then said, 'This means going outside the ship.'

'I'm sorry,' Hal replied. 'I thought you knew.'

'I probably did a year ago,' Bowman said. 'Anyway, it looks simple enough. We only have to unlock a cover and put in a new unit.'

'That suits me fine,' said Poole, who was responsible for routine work outside. 'It'll be something different.'

Chapter 22   Leaving the Ship

Poole put on his pressure suit and climbed inside the small vehicle designed for work outside *Discovery*. It was round in shape and had a large window in front which gave the operator an excellent view. *Discovery* carried three of these vehicles, known as Anna, Betty and Clara.

Poole spent ten minutes carefully checking the controls. Then, when he was completely satisfied, he spoke to Hal over the radio. Though Bowman was watching in the Control Room, he would not get involved unless something went obviously wrong.

'This is Betty. Start pumping operation.'

'Pumping operation started,' repeated Hal.

At once Poole could hear the noise of the pumps as air was taken out of the room. Then the thin metal of the vehicle's skin began to make small noises under the pressure. After five minutes, Hal reported:

'Pumping finished.'

Poole made a final check of the instruments. Everything was perfectly normal.

'Open outside door,' he ordered.

Hal repeated the instruction, and the walls of the ship slid apart. Poole felt the vehicle shake slightly as the last of the air rushed out into space. Then he was looking at the stars.

'Send vehicle out.'

Very slowly, the metal bar from which Betty was hanging pushed itself out through the open door, until the vehicle was just outside the ship.

Poole pulled back slightly on the main jet control, and Betty slid off the metal bar. He now had no connection with *Discovery* – not even a safety line.

He let the vehicle move out for thirty metres, then slowed her down and turned back towards the ship, approaching the antenna from behind in case he interrupted the radio signal and caused a short loss of contact with Earth.

He saw the small metal plate that covered the AE 35 unit. It was held in place by four connectors, and should not be difficult to remove. However, he could not do the job from inside the vehicle. He spoke to Bowman on the radio, and they discussed what needed to be done. Outside the ship there were no small mistakes.

He parked Betty on top of the ship about six metres away from the antenna. Then he checked the systems of his pressure suit and, when he was quite satisfied, let the air out of the vehicle. There was one more thing to do before he got out. He pushed down a switch so that Betty was now controlled by Hal. Though he was still connected to the vehicle by a very strong safety line, even the best lines could fail. He would look a fool if he needed his vehicle and was unable to call it to his assistance by passing instructions to Hal.

The door of the vehicle swung open, and he moved slowly out into the silence of space. Never move quickly – stop and think – these were the rules for working outside the ship.

With a gentle push, he sent himself towards the big round dish. His double shadow, produced by Betty's two front lights, danced across the skin of the ship. He stopped himself from banging into the antenna by pushing out an arm. Quickly he hooked his safety line on.

He studied the four connectors for a moment, then took a tool from the belt of his suit and started to undo them. He had to push against his safety line to stay in place, but they came off without any trouble. The metal cover was a little hard to move, but after a few knocks it came loose. He fixed it to one of the antenna supports.

Now he could see the AE 35 unit. It was about the same size and shape as a postcard, and it had a small handle so it could easily be removed. But it was still controlling the direction of the antenna. If he removed it now, the dish would swing round to its central position, to point along the length of the ship. It might even crash into him as it turned. Also, this would cut off contact with Earth.

'Hal,' Poole called out over the radio. 'I am going to remove the unit. Switch off all control power to the antenna system.'

'Antenna control power off,' Hal said.

'Right. I'm pulling the unit out now.'

The card slipped out without any difficulty. Within a minute, its spare was in place.

But Poole was taking no chances. He pushed himself gently away from the antenna, just in case the big dish went wild when the power was switched back on. Then he called Hal again.

'The new unit should be working. Switch control power on.'

'Power on,' Hal said. The antenna didn't move.

'Unit is working,' Hal said, ten seconds later. In that time he had carried out as many tests as a small army of human inspectors.

'Fine,' said Poole. 'I'm now replacing the cover.'

This was often the most dangerous part of a job outside. Mistakes were often made when people had to tidy up before their return to the ship. But Frank Poole was a careful man – that was one reason why he had been chosen for the mission. He took his time, and though one of the connectors almost got away from him, he caught it before it had travelled more than a couple of metres.

Fifteen minutes later, he was moving the vehicle back through the open doors of the ship, quietly confident that the job would not need to be done again.

He was, however, sadly mistaken.

Chapter 23   Sickness

'Do you mean,' Frank Poole said, more surprised than annoyed, 'that I did all that work for nothing?'

'It seems like it,' answered Bowman. 'The unit's working perfectly. It passed every test.'

The two men were standing in the tiny workshop-laboratory in the central living area. The thin, card-sized plate of the AE 35 unit lay on the table, connected to a number of wires which led to a small screen.

'Try it yourself,' said Bowman.

Poole pushed the *TEST* button. At once, the screen flashed the message, *UNIT OK.*

'What do you think?' Poole said.

'Maybe Hal's own testing system made a mistake. It's possible.'

'It's more likely that there's a fault with this thing,' Poole said, pointing to the screen. 'Anyway, better safe than sorry. I'm glad we replaced the unit.'

Bowman took out the AE 35 and held it up to the light. The thin material was covered with wiring, so it looked like a piece of modern art.

'We can't take any chances – this is our connection with Earth. I'll write a report then drop this in a box. Somebody else can worry about it when we get home.'

But the worrying began a long time before that, with the next message from Earth.

'This is Mission Control. We appear to have a slight problem.'

'Your report that there is nothing wrong with the AE 35 unit agrees with our opinion. It seems more likely that your computer made a mistake. This is not a reason to worry, but we would like you to watch out for any other changes from normal performance. We have suspected several other irregularities in the past few days, but none have seemed important enough to need correction.

'We are running more tests with both our 9000s, and will report as soon as results are available. If necessary, we may disconnect your 9000 temporarily for testing and pass over control to one of our computers. The time difference will introduce problems, but our studies show that Earth control is perfectly satisfactory at this stage of the mission.

'This is Mission Control. Message ends.'

Frank Poole, who was in command when the message came in, thought about this in silence. Then he went to see Bowman, who was pouring himself some coffee in the kitchen. Poole said good morning – they both still used Earth time – and helped himself to a cup.

'What's the problem?' said Bowman. Any change from the normal routine meant that something was not quite right.

'Well ...' Poole answered slowly. 'We've just had a message from Mission Control.' He lowered his voice. 'We may have a slight case of space sickness on board.'

Perhaps Bowman was not fully awake because it took him several seconds to understand. Then he said, 'Oh, I see. What else did they tell you?'

'That there was no reason to worry. And that they were considering a temporary switch-over to Earth Control, while they checked things out.'

They both knew, of course, that Hal was hearing every word, but they could not help speaking indirectly. Hal was their colleague, and they did not want to embarrass him. But it did not yet seem necessary to discuss the matter in private.

Bowman finished his breakfast in silence, while Poole played with the empty coffee-container. They were both thinking hard, but there was nothing more to say.

Whatever happened, the atmosphere on the ship had changed a little. There was tension in the air and, for the first time, a feeling that something might be going wrong.

Discovery was no longer a happy ship.

Chapter 24 Breakdown

Poole was asleep, and Bowman was reading in the Control Room, when Hal announced, 'Dave, I have a report for you.'

'What is it?'

'We have another bad AE 35 unit. My tests suggest failure within twenty-four hours.'

Bowman put down his book and stared at the computer screen. He knew, of course, that Hal was not really *there*, whatever that meant. But it seemed polite to look at the screen when speaking to him.

'I can't understand it, Hal. *Two* units can't go wrong within a couple of days.'

'It does seem strange, Dave. But I am certain that the unit will fail.'

'Let me see how things look now.'

He knew that this would prove nothing, but he wanted time to think. The familiar view of Earth appeared on the screen. It was perfectly centred on the cross-wires, as Bowman knew it must be. If there had been any break in communication, the alarm would already have sounded.

'Have you any idea,' he said, 'what's causing the fault?'

It was unusual for Hal to pause so long. Then he answered: 'Not really, Dave. As I reported earlier, I can't say exactly where the trouble is.'

'You're quite certain,' said Bowman, cautiously, 'that you haven't made a mistake? You know we tested the other AE 35 unit thoroughly, and there was nothing wrong with it.'

'Yes, I know that, but I'm sure there is a fault. If it's not in the unit, it may be in one of the other systems.'

That was possible, though it might be very difficult to prove – until a breakdown happened and showed them where the trouble was.

'Well, I'll report it to Mission Control and we'll see what they advise.' He paused, but there was no reaction. 'Hal,' he continued, 'is something worrying you – something that possibly caused this problem?'

Again there was that unusual delay. Then Hal answered, 'I'm not sure how to say this nicely, Dave, but ... I'm not a human being; I'm a computer. I don't make mistakes.'

◆

When the face of Dr Simonson, the Chief Programmer, appeared on the screen, Poole and Bowman knew this could only mean trouble.

'This is Mission Control. We have looked into your AE 35 difficulty, and both of our Hal 9000s are in agreement. The report you gave of a second failure only makes us more certain.

'The fault does not lie in the AE 35, and there is no need to replace it again. The fault is in the connecting wires, and this suggests a problem with programming. We can only repair this if you

50

disconnect your 9000 and switch to Earth Control. You will therefore take the following steps, beginning at 22.00 Ship Time ...'

The voice died away. At the same time, the alarm system sounded, and then Hal's voice said, 'Condition Yellow! Condition Yellow!'

'What's wrong?' Bowman said, though he had already guessed the answer.

'The AE 35 unit has failed, as I said it would.'

Chapter 25   First Man to Saturn

As he had done on his previous trip outside, Frank Poole parked Betty about six metres away from the antenna and switched control over to Hal before opening up.

'Going outside now,' he reported to Bowman.

There was silence for some time, as Poole moved slowly towards the antenna. Then he called out, 'Hal, there's too much shadow here – swing the vehicle lights twenty degrees to the left – thanks – that's OK.'

Somewhere in Bowman's mind, a warning bell started to ring. There was something strange, and it took him a few seconds to realize what it was.

Hal had obeyed the order, but had not said a word. That was unusual. When Poole had finished, they should discuss this . . .

Outside, Poole removed the cover, then pulled the little unit out of its place and held it up to the sunlight.

'Here it is,' he said. 'It still looks perfectly OK to me.'

Then he stopped. A sudden movement had caught his eye – out here, where no movement was possible.

He looked up in alarm. The pattern of light from the vehicle's two main lights had started to move around him. His first thought was that Betty had moved away from the ship. But no – she was coming straight towards him, under full power.

The sight was so unbelievable that he said nothing; he did not even try to move away. Then he recovered enough to shout, 'Hal! Full braking . . .'

Inside *Discovery*, that shout over the radio made Bowman jump violently.

'What's wrong, Frank?' he called.

Then, outside the wide observation windows, something moved. He saw Betty, travelling almost at full speed, heading out towards the stars.

'Hal!' he cried. 'What's wrong? Full braking power on Betty! Full braking power!'

Nothing happened, and then, pulled behind her on the end of the safety line, appeared a spacesuit. One look was enough to tell Bowman the worst. It was the soft shape of a suit that had lost its pressure and was open to vacuum.

Within five minutes the vehicle and its satellite had disappeared among the stars. For a long time, David Bowman stared after it into the emptiness that stretched so many millions of kilometres ahead. Only one thought kept hammering in his brain.

Frank Poole would be the first of all men to reach Saturn.

Chapter 26   Conversation with Hal

Bowman was sitting in the little kitchen, a half-finished cup of coffee in his hand. He did not remember making his way there from the Control Room.

Directly opposite him was one of the glass fish-eyes that Hal used to see around the ship. Bowman rose slowly to his feet and walked towards it.

'It's a pity about Frank,' Hal said.

'Yes,' Bowman answered, after a long pause. 'It is.'

'He was an excellent crew member.'

Finding the coffee still in his hand, Bowman took a slow mouthful. Had it been an accident, caused by some failure of the vehicle controls? Or was it a mistake by Hal?

The only other possibility was that Hal had killed Frank. Bowman found the idea strange, but he had to consider it. If it was true, he was in terrible danger.

His next act was written into the mission orders, but he was not sure how safe it was. If either crew member was killed, the other man had to replace him at once from the hibernators. Whitehead was first on the list, then Kaminski, then Hunter. The waking up process was under Hal's control, so he could act if both his human colleagues were dead.

But Bowman could also take control if he wanted to. He also felt that one human companion was not enough. He decided to wake up all three of the hibernators. In the difficult weeks and months ahead, he might need all the help he could get.

'Hal,' he said. 'Give me hibernation control – on all the units.'

'*All* of them, Dave?'

'Yes.'

'May I remind you that only one replacement is needed.'

'I know that, but I prefer to do it this way.'

'Are you sure it's necessary to wake up *any* of them, Dave? We can manage very well by ourselves.'

This was new, and it made Bowman even more nervous. Hal knew that Whitehead had to be woken. He was suggesting a great change in mission planning.

'Since an emergency has developed,' Bowman said, 'I want as much help as possible. So please let me have control of the hibernators.'

'If you still really want to wake up the whole crew, I can handle it myself. There's no need for you to worry.'

Bowman felt he was caught in a bad dream. It was like being questioned by the police about a crime of which he knew nothing – knowing that one careless word would lead to disaster. He became angry.

'Hal, unless you obey my instructions, I shall be forced to disconnect you. Now give me control!'

Hal's surrender was as total as it was unexpected.

'OK, Dave,' he said. 'You're certainly the boss. I was only trying to do what I thought best.'

◆

As Bowman slid open the door of Whitehead's hibernator, he felt the cold air strike him in the face. The screen, a copy of the one in the Control Room, showed that everything was perfectly normal. He pressed the button on the Wakener. There was no sound, no sign that anything had started to happen, but the curves on the screen began to change their shape. In about ten minutes, Whitehead would wake up.

And then two things happened at the same time. Both were very small changes, hardly noticeable, but after three months on *Discovery* Bowman knew his ship well.

First, the lights became slightly unsteady for a moment, which always happened when any piece of equipment started up. But he could think of no equipment which would suddenly start working at this point.

Then he heard the far-off sound of an electric motor. To Bowman, every motor on the ship had its own individual sound, and he recognized this one immediately.

The airlock doors, which last opened for Frank's flight to his death, were opening again.

Chapter 27   Hal's Secret

Since he had first become conscious, in that laboratory on Earth, all Hal's powers and skills had been pointed in one direction. The only reason for his existence was to complete the mission.

But since the ship had left Earth, he had been troubled by a secret he could not share with Poole and Bowman. And the time was fast approaching when his colleagues would learn that he had deceived them.

The three hibernators already knew the truth, but they could not talk in their sleep. But Poole and Bowman had not been told. It was a secret that was very hard to hide, because it affected a person's attitudes and their voice. So the two active members of the crew, who were in regular contact with Earth, would only learn the mission's full purpose when they needed to know.

The reason for this meant nothing to Hal. He knew a secret, and he wanted to tell it to Poole and Bowman. He couldn't tell it, so he had begun to worry. He had also begun to make mistakes, though he could not admit this to himself.

But, worse than any tension, he had been threatened with disconnection. To Hal, this was the same as death. Because he had never slept, he did not know that it was possible to wake up again.

So he would protect himself, with all the weapons at his command. And then, following the orders that had been given to him in case of a serious emergency, he would continue the mission alone.

Chapter 28   In Vacuum

A moment later, Bowman could hear a great noise as the air began to leave the ship. The first winds pulled at his body, then suddenly he was fighting to stay on his feet.

He looked back only once at Whitehead. There was nothing he could do now for him or any of the others. He had to save himself.

Now the wind was rushing past him, carrying with it loose pieces of clothing, sheets of paper, food from the kitchen, anything that had not been fixed in place. He had a moment to see this, then the lights went out and he was in screaming darkness.

Almost immediately the emergency lamps came on, filling the ship with a faint blue light. Now it was becoming difficult to breathe, and the pressure was dropping. He knew he could expect only about fifteen seconds before his brain began to die. Fortunately, the wind was slowing down. He knew there was an emergency shelter just along the passage. He ran towards it and pulled the door to him. It moved and he fell inside, using the weight of his body to close it behind him.

The tiny room was just large enough to hold one man – and a spacesuit. Near the ceiling was a lever labelled *OXYGEN*. Bowman caught hold of it and, with his last strength, pulled it down.

For long moments he stood breathing hard, while the pressure in the little room rose around him. When his body returned to normal, he stood and listened. The ship was silent now, airless, a dead thing in space.

Bowman got into the spacesuit. It seemed a pity to waste the oxygen in the room, but he knew what had to be done, and there was no point in waiting. He pressed a button that allowed it to escape. Then, when the pressure on each side of the door was equal, he opened it and walked back to the hibernation room.

He looked at Whitehead first. He had thought that a hibernating man showed no sign of life, but he was wrong. Though it was impossible to describe, there was a difference between hibernation and death. The red lights and straight lines on the screen proved what he had already guessed.

It was the same with the other two. He had never known them very well; he would never know them now.

He was the only living thing on the ship, but he knew that he was not alone. To be safe, he must be even lonelier.

◆

The door was not locked, but there were a number of warning notices on it. Obviously, anybody who opened it had to have a good reason. Bowman pulled on the handle and entered the small room.

He had been here only once before, while Hal was being built into the ship. He had quite forgotten that there was a glass fish-eye watching the neat rows of electronic units.

'It seems that something has gone wrong, Dave.'

Bowman took no notice. He was carefully studying the little labels on the units, checking his plan of action.

'Hello, Dave,' said Hal. 'Have you found the trouble?'

This would be a very difficult operation. He could not simply cut off Hal's power supply, because he needed Hal to run the ship. Without him, *Discovery* would be mechanically dead. The only answer was to cut out the higher centres of Hal's brain, and to leave the purely automatic control systems in place.

'I think there has been a failure in the airlock doors,' Hal remarked. 'Lucky you weren't killed.'

Bowman undid the locking bar on the unit that allowed Hal to think about the results of his actions. He pulled the unit out and let it float across the room.

'Hey, Dave,' said Hal. 'What are you doing?'

There was a series of units that let Hal feel good about himself. Bowman pulled them out one by one.

'Listen, Dave,' said Hal. 'I've got years of experience. A lot of work has gone into making me what I am.'

Bowman started on the intelligence units.

'Dave,' said Hal. 'I don't understand why you are doing this to me ... I have great enthusiasm for the mission ... You are destroying my mind ... Don't you understand? ... I will become childish ... I will become nothing ...'

This is harder than I expected, thought Bowman. I am destroying the only conscious creature in my universe.

'I am a Hal 9000 computer, Production Number 3. I was built at the Hal factory in Urbana, Illinois on January 12, 1997. The rain in Spain is mainly in the ... Dave – are you still there? Two times two is ... er ... 4 ... I seem to be having some difficulty ...'

The voice stopped so suddenly that Bowman froze for a moment, his hand still holding one of the remaining memory units. Then, unexpectedly, Hal spoke again.

The speech was much slower, and the words had a dead, mechanical sound. They did not sound at all like they came from Hal.

'Good ... morning ... Doctor ... Chandra ... This ... is ... Hal ... I ... am ... ready ... for ... my ... first ... lesson ... today ...'

Bowman pulled out the last unit, and Hal was silent for ever.

Chapter 29   Alone

Like a tiny complicated toy, the ship floated in space. There was no sign of any life on board. In fact, there were two signs that all life had ended – the airlock doors were wide open, and coming out from them was a cloud of rubbish that was already several kilometres long.

But there was still power on board. A faint blue light was shining from the windows. And now, at last, there was movement.

A long object covered in cloth came out of the airlock and floated away. A moment later it was followed by another – and then a third.

Half an hour passed, and then one of the space vehicles came out through the airlock. It moved slowly round the ship and landed near the base of the antenna. A space-suited figure got out of it, worked there for a few minutes, then returned to the vehicle. After a time the vehicle made its way back to the airlock and re-entered the ship.

Nothing happened for over an hour. Then the airlock doors closed and, a little later, the full lighting system came on. Then the great bowl of the antenna began to move, turning round to face the back of the ship.

Inside *Discovery*, David Bowman carefully pointed the antenna towards Earth. There was no automatic control now, but he could hold it steady for a few minutes. It would be over an hour before his words reached Earth, and another hour before any reply could reach him.

It was difficult to imagine what answer Earth could possibly send, except a sympathetic 'Goodbye'.

Chapter 30   The Secret

Heywood Floyd looked very tired, but he was doing his best to give confidence to the lonely man on the other side of the Solar System.

'First of all, Dr Bowman,' he began, 'we must congratulate you on the way you handled an extremely difficult situation. We believe we know the cause of your HAL 9000's problem, but we'll discuss that later. For the moment, we want to give you every possible assistance, so that you can complete your mission.

'And now I must tell you its real purpose. We were going to

tell you all the facts as you approached Saturn, but things have changed. You need to know now.

'Two years ago we discovered the first proof of intelligent life outside the Earth. An object made of black material, three metres high, was found buried in the crater Tycho. Here it is.'

A photograph of TMA-1, with men in spacesuits standing beside it, appeared on the screen. Bowman leaned forwards in open-mouthed surprise. Like everybody else interested in space, he had half-expected something like this all his life.

Heywood Floyd reappeared on the screen.

'The most amazing thing about this object is its age. Everything we know about it suggests that it is three million years old. You would expect, then, that it is completely lifeless. However, soon after lunar sunrise, it gave out a very powerful radio signal. We were able to follow this with great accuracy. It was aimed exactly at Saturn.

'When we thought later about what happened, we decided that the object was either powered by the Sun, or at least started up by the Sun. We felt this because it sent its signal immediately after sunrise, when it was in daylight for the first time in three million years.

'The question now is why a sun-powered object was buried ten metres underground. We've examined dozens of theories, and the favourite one is the simplest. It is also the most worrying.

'You hide a sun-powered object in darkness only if you want to know when it is brought out into the light. In other words, the object may be some kind of alarm bell. And we have made it ring . . .

'We don't know whether the creatures that put it there still exist. If they do, they may be dangerous. Whether they are or not, we need to make preparations. But we cannot do anything until we know more about them.

'Your mission, then, is much more than a voyage of discovery. You are going into what may be a dangerous area to find out what you can. It may seem unbelievable that any life-forms could exist on Saturn. But life may be possible on one or more of its moons. We are particularly interested in its eighth moon, Japetus, and we may ask you to look closely at it.

'At the moment, we do not know whether to hope or fear. We do not know if, out on the moons of Saturn, you will meet with good or evil – or only with ruins a thousand times older than Troy.'*

PART FIVE   The Moons of Saturn

Chapter 31   Survival

Work is the best cure for any shock, and Bowman now had plenty to do. As quickly as possible, he had to get *Discovery* working properly again.

Life Support was the most important thing. Much oxygen had been lost, but there was enough left to provide for a single man. The computers on Earth could now do many of the jobs that Hal had done. It would take them quite a long time to react to a change in conditions, but none of the work was urgent.

Bowman went back and closed the doors of the hibernators. It had been the worst job, getting the bodies out. He was glad that they had been colleagues and not friends. Now all three of them would reach Saturn before him – but not before Frank Poole. Somehow, Bowman was pleased about this.

---

*Troy: an ancient city in what is now Turkey. People believe it was destroyed in 1184 BC.

He did not try to check if the hibernator was still working. One day, his life might depend on it, but many things might happen before then. He tried to avoid thinking about such distant problems, and concentrated on immediate ones. Slowly he cleaned up the ship, checking that its systems were still running smoothly and discussing technical difficulties with Earth. During those first few weeks he did not get much sleep, and he did not think very much about the great mystery that lay ahead.

At last, when the ship settled down into its automatic routine – though it still needed a lot of his attention – Bowman had time to study the reports sent to him from Earth. Again and again he played back the recording made when TMA-1 woke up and greeted the dawn for the first time in three million years.

Since that moment, the black object had done nothing. No attempt had been made to cut into it. The scientists were naturally cautious, and they were also afraid of the possible results.

One strange, and perhaps unimportant, feature of the block had led to endless argument. It was roughly three metres high by 1.3m across by about 0.3m deep. When its size was measured with great care, the relationship between the three figures was exactly 1 to 4 to 9. This remained true to the limits of accurate measurement. It was also true that no technical process on Earth could shape a block of *any* material so accurately. In a way, this was as amazing as any other feature of TMA-1.

Chapter 32   Life in Space

Apart from quick meals in the kitchen, Bowman spent almost all his time in the Control Room. He slept in his seat so he could see any trouble as soon as the first signs of it appeared on the screen. Under instructions from Mission Control, he had built several emergency systems which were working quite well. It even seemed possible that he would live until the *Discovery* reached Saturn. Of course the ship would get there whether he was alive or not.

Though he had little time for sight-seeing, there were views through *Discovery*'s windows that often made it difficult to concentrate on the problems of survival. He could see many stars, but Alpha Centauri always seemed to attract Bowman's eyes and mind when he looked into space. This was the nearest of all stars beyond the Solar System, but its light had taken four years to reach him.

There was obviously some connection between TMA-1 and Saturn, but no one believed that the builders of the rock could possibly come from there. As a place to live, Saturn was even more dangerous than Jupiter.

But if these creatures had come from beyond the Solar System, how had they travelled the enormous distance from the nearest star?

Scientists reminded people that *Discovery*, the fastest ship ever designed, would take twenty thousand years to reach Alpha Centauri. Even if, at some time in the future, ships' engines improved greatly, in the end there would still be the problem of the speed of light. No material object could go faster than this. Therefore the builders of TMA-1 had shared the same sun as Man, and since they had made no appearance in modern times, they had probably died out.

A small number of scientists disagreed. Even if it took centuries to travel from star to star, they said, this might not stop really keen explorers. Hibernation, as used on *Discovery*, was one possible answer. Also, why should we believe that all intelligent life lived for as short a time as Man? There might be creatures in the Universe to whom a thousand-year voyage might be uninteresting, but certainly possible.

There was also discussion about what such creatures would

look like. Some believed that the human shape of two legs, two arms and a head at the top was so sensible that it was hard to think of a better one. Others said that the human body was just a result of chance over millions of years. If circumstances had been different, it would not have developed in the same way.

There were other thinkers who held even stranger views. They felt that as soon as it was technically possible, bodies would be replaced by machines. On Earth this process was starting to happen, with the replacement of some parts of the body which had stopped working.

And eventually, even brains might go. The war between mind and machine might be settled at last with a true partnership.

But was even this the end? Some had even more extreme views and argued that the mind might eventually free itself from all physical limits. The mechanical body, like the flesh-and-blood one, might only be a stage on the way to something which, long ago, men called 'spirit'.

And if there was anything beyond *that*, its name could only be God.

Chapter 33   Ambassador

During the last three months, David Bowman had become so used to living alone that it was hard to remember any other existence. He had passed beyond sadness and even doubt, and had accepted his new life.

But he had not passed beyond curiosity, and sometimes the thought of where he was going filled him with a feeling of great power. He was an ambassador for the whole human race, but his actions during the next few weeks might shape its whole future.

So he kept himself neat and tidy, and he never missed a shave.

Mission Control, he knew, was watching him closely for any signs of unusual behaviour. He did not want to show them any.

However, some things did change. He could not stand silence. Except when he was sleeping, or talking to Earth, he kept the ship's sound system turned up high.

At first, needing the company of the human voice, he listened to plays or poetry readings from *Discovery*'s enormous library. The problems they dealt with, though, seemed so far away, or so simple, that he soon lost patience with them.

So he switched to music. Sibelius, Tchaikovsky and Berlioz lasted a few weeks; Beethoven lasted longer. But one by one he left them as their emotional power became too much for him. In the end he found peace, as so many others had done, in the mathematical exactness of Bach.

And so the *Discovery* drove on towards Saturn, ringing with the cool music of the eighteenth century, the frozen thoughts of a brain that had been dust for twice a hundred years.

◆

Although it was still sixteen million kilometres away, Saturn already appeared larger than the Moon as seen from Earth. It was a wonderful sight; through the telescope it was unbelievable.

The system of its rings, so enormous but as flat as thin paper, were like a work of art. They were not solid, but made of countless numbers of small pieces, perhaps the remains of a destroyed moon. Bowman spent hours looking at them, knowing that they would not last for long and had appeared as recently as three million years ago.

It was rather odd that they had been born at the same time as the human race.

Chapter 34   The Orbiting Ice

Discovery was now deep inside the system of Saturn's moons. The ship had passed inside the wide orbit of Phoebe. Ahead of it now lay Japetus, Hyperion, Titan, Rhea, Dione, Tethys, Encaladus, Mimas — and the rings themselves. All the moons showed great detail through the telescope, and Bowman had sent back to Earth as many photographs as he could take.

But Japetus held most of his attention. One half of the satellite — which, like its companions, turned the same face always towards Saturn — was extremely dark and showed very little surface detail. In complete contrast, the other was largely covered by a brilliant white oval, about six hundred kilometres long and three hundred wide. It sat in the middle of Japetus, with its narrow ends pointing to the poles. It was so even and so sharp-edged that it looked as if it had been painted there. Because it looked so flat, Bowman wondered if it might be a lake of frozen liquid, but that would not explain its even appearance.

However, Bowman had little time to study it in detail; the most dangerous part of the voyage was rapidly approaching. As it flew past Jupiter, the ship had used the planet's gravity to increase her speed. Now she must do the opposite. She had to slow down as much as possible so she did not escape from the Solar System and fly on to the stars. Her present path was designed to trap her, so she would become another moon of Saturn, going round on a three-million-kilometre-long oval orbit. At its near point she would come close to the planet; at its far point she would touch the orbit of Japetus.

The computers back on Earth, though their information was always three hours late, had told Bowman that everything was in order. The ship had to fly over the dark side of Saturn, out of radio contact with Earth and losing speed all the time, then rise up again into the sunlight and fly on for another three million kilometres. It would take her fourteen days to make that climb, crossing the paths of all the inside moons. Then she would meet Japetus.

If she failed, she would fall back towards Saturn and repeat her twenty-eight day orbit. But the next time round, Japetus would be far away, almost on the other side of the planet.

It was true that they would meet again, when the orbits of ship and moon came together for a second time. But that would be so many years ahead that, whatever happened, Bowman knew he would not see it.

Chapter 35   The Eye of Japetus

When Bowman had first seen Japetus, the curious bright oval area had been partly in shadow. Now, as the moon moved slowly along its seventy-nine day orbit, it was coming into the full light of day.

As he watched it grow, Bowman began to have a worrying feeling. He never mentioned it to Mission Control because he did not want them to think he was going mad. Perhaps he was; he had almost made himself believe that the bright oval was an enormous empty eye, staring at him as he approached. But it was not completely empty. When the ship was eighty thousand kilometres out, and Japetus was twice as large as the Earth's familiar Moon, he noticed a tiny black spot at the exact centre of the oval. However there was no time, then, for any detailed examination. The meeting-point was getting close.

For the last time, *Discovery*'s main engines started up. David Bowman felt a sense of pride, and of sadness. These engines had brought the ship here from Earth with total efficiency. Soon there would be no more fuel, and then *Discovery* would be as dead as an asteroid, a helpless prisoner of gravity. Even when the rescue ship finally arrived a few years into the future, it would not be economical to refuel her. She would continue to orbit, empty and alone.

The whistle of the main jets died away. Only the side jets continued to move *Discovery* gently into orbit. Then even they shut down. The ship was now circling Japetus at a height of eighty kilometres.

Discovery had become a satellite of a satellite.

Chapter 36　Big Brother

'I'm coming round to the daylight side again, and it's just as I reported on the last orbit. This place seems to have only two kinds of surface material. The black stuff looks *burnt* – very like burnt toast.

'I still can't make any sense of the white area. It has a very sharp edge, and there are no surface details at all. Picture a sea of frozen milk – though sometimes I feel that it's moving slowly.

'. . . I'm over the white area again, on my third orbit. This time I hope to pass closer to that mark I noticed at its centre, on my way in. If my calculations are correct, I'll go within eighty kilometres of it – whatever it is.

'. . . Yes, there's something ahead, just where I calculated. It's coming over the horizon – and so is Saturn. I'll move to the telescope . . .

'Hello! – it looks like some kind of building – completely black. No windows or other features. Just a big object standing . . . at least a kilometre high. It reminds me – of course! *It's just like the thing you found on the Moon!* This is TMA-1's big brother!'

Chapter 37   Experiment

Call it the Star Gate.

For three million years it had circled Saturn, waiting for a meeting that might never come. When it was created, a moon was destroyed, and the broken pieces still orbited the planet.

Now the long wait was ending. On another world, intelligence had been born and was escaping from its home. An ancient experiment was almost at an end.

The creatures who had begun that experiment, so long ago, had not been human. But they were flesh and blood. And as soon as they were able to, they flew to the stars.

In their explorations, they met with life in many forms. And when they found it had some intelligence, they encouraged its growth. When the explorers came to Earth, they made changes to many types of animal. They would not know, for at least a million years, which of their experiments would succeed. But there was no need for them to wait and watch. The servants they had left behind would do that for them.

As time passed, those first explorers of Earth went through many changes themselves. As soon as they could build machines that were better than their bodies, they left their bodies and became machines. In time, they learned to store knowledge in the structure of space itself. Then they freed themselves from the machines and turned into creatures of pure energy.

Now they were lords of the Galaxy, and beyond the reach of time. They could move as they wanted among the stars. But despite their godlike powers, they had not completely forgotten their beginning.

And they still watched the experiments that had been started so long ago.

Chapter 38   The Watcher

'There's been no reaction to my signals, and every time I fly over, I'm a bit further away from TMA-2. At the moment my closest approach is a hundred kilometres. That will increase slowly as Japetus turns beneath me, then it will drop back to zero. I'll pass directly over it in thirty days, but by that time it will be in darkness.

'So I'd like you to agree to this plan. I want to leave the ship in one of the space vehicles and take a close look. If it seems safe, I'll land beside it – or even on top of it.

'I'm sure this is the only thing to do. I've come more than a billion kilometres – I don't want to be stopped by the last hundred.'

◆

For weeks the Star Gate had watched the approaching ship. Its makers had prepared it for many things, and this was one of them. It watched, then it listened to the ship's signals, but it did nothing.

There was a long pause, then it saw that something was falling down towards it. It searched its memory and made the decisions it was built to make.

Beneath the cold light of Saturn, the Star Gate woke its sleeping powers.

Chapter 39   Into the Eye

Discovery looked just as he had last seen her from space, floating in lunar orbit with the Moon taking up half the sky. Now he was leaving, perhaps for the last time, the metal world that had been his home for so many months. Even if he never returned, the ship would continue to send signals back to Earth, until finally its electrical systems failed.

And if he did return? Well, he could stay alive for a few more months. But that was all, because the hibernation systems were useless with no computer to operate them. He could not possibly continue to live until *Discovery II* arrived in four or five years time.

He put these thoughts behind him as the black block of TMA-2 climbed above the horizon. He turned the vehicle right round and used the engines to slow his speed. He was still about eight kilometres high now, and heading straight for the enormous black object. It was as featureless as the flat surface below him, and until now he had not realized how enormous it really was. And as far as could be seen, its sizes had exactly the same 1 to 4 to 9 relationship as those of TMA-1.

'I'm only five kilometres away now. Still no sign of activity – nothing on any of the instruments. The sides and top seem absolutely smooth and polished. Now I'm directly over it, about a hundred and fifty metres up. I'm going to land. It's certainly solid enough.

'Just a minute – that's odd . . .'

Bowman's voice died away. He was not frightened; he simply could not describe what he was seeing. He had been hanging above a black block, but now the top of it seemed to be moving away from him, down to the surface of Japetus, and then lower. It was exactly like looking at a drawing of a square box, where suddenly the near side can become the far side. Now it seemed he was looking straight down a black hole in the ground. And, even more strange, although its sides went down for a long way, they never seemed to get closer together.

David Bowman had time for just one broken sentence, which the scientists waiting in Mission Control, fourteen million kilometres away, never forgot:

'The thing's hollow – it goes on for ever – and – oh my God – *it's full of stars!*'

Chapter 40   Exit

The Star Gate opened. The Star Gate closed.

In a moment of time too short to be measured, Space turned and twisted on itself.

Then Japetus was alone again, as it had been for three million years – alone, except for an empty ship, sending back to its makers messages which they could not believe or understand.

PART SIX   Through the Star Gate

Chapter 41   Grand Central

David Bowman seemed to be dropping down a hole several thousand metres deep. He was moving faster and faster – but the far end never changed its size, and remained always at the same distance from him.

Time was also behaving strangely, as he realized when he looked at the vehicle's small clock. Normally, the tenth-of-a-second window moved past so quickly that it was almost impossible for him to read the numbers. Now the numbers seemed to be slowing down. At last, the counter stopped between five and six.

But he could still think, and watch, as the black walls moved past him at a speed he could not even begin to guess. He was not at all surprised, or afraid. He had travelled those millions of kilometres in search of a mystery, and now it seemed that the mystery was coming to him.

The end of the passage, which had stood still for so long, began to move towards him. For a moment he wondered if he had fallen right through Japetus. But when the vehicle came out into the light, he knew this place was unlike any known world.

It was big, perhaps much bigger than Earth, but all the surface that Bowman could see was covered with large artificial shapes, some kilometres long on each side. And at the centre of many of those were large black holes — like the one that he had come out from.

The sky above, at first, looked soft and milky-white. But as he looked closer, he realized that it was covered with many small black spots. They reminded Bowman of something so familiar, but so crazy that for a time he refused to accept the idea. Those black holes in the white sky were stars. It was like looking at a photographic negative of the Milky Way.*

Where am I? Bowman asked himself. But even as he asked the question, he knew that he could never know the answer. It seemed that Space had been turned inside out: this was not a place for Man. Although the vehicle was comfortably warm, he felt suddenly cold and started to shake.

Something was coming over the horizon. At first it looked like a circle, but that was because it was moving directly towards him. As it approached and passed beneath him, he saw that it was tube-shaped, and several hundred metres long. It was pointed at each end, but there was no sign of a jet engine.

He moved his eyes to another screen to watch the thing drop behind him. It had ignored him completely, and now it was falling out of the sky, down towards one of those thousands of great holes. A few seconds later it dived into the planet, and Bowman was alone again.

Then he saw that he was sinking down towards the surface. One of the holes grew larger beneath him, and then the empty sky closed above him. The clock slowed and stopped. Once again his vehicle was falling between black walls towards another distant group of stars. But now he was sure he was not returning

*Milky Way: a galaxy of about 100,000 stars, including the Sun.

73

to the Solar System, and suddenly he realized what this place must be.

It was like some kind of enormous crossroads, allowing the traffic of the stars to move into different areas of space and time. He was passing through a Grand Central Station* of the Galaxy.

Chapter 42   A Different Sky

Far ahead, the walls of the hole were becoming faintly light again. And then the darkness suddenly ended, as the tiny vehicle shot upwards into a sky lit up with stars.

He was back in space as he knew it, but a single look told him he was light-centuries from Earth. He did not even try to find some of the familiar patterns of stars. Perhaps none of them had ever been seen without the help of a telescope.

Most were concentrated in a shining belt which completely circled the sky. Bowman wondered if this was his own galaxy, seen from a point much closer to its shining, crowded centre.

He hoped that it was; then he would not be so far from home. But this, he realized at once, was a childish thought. He was so far from the Solar System that it made little difference whether he was in his own galaxy or the most distant one that any telescope had ever found.

He looked back to see the thing from which he was rising, and had another shock. There was no surface covered with great patterns, nor any copy of Japetus. There was nothing – except a black shadow, like an open door into a dark room. As he watched, that black shadow slowly filled with stars, as if a hole in space had been repaired.

The vehicle was turning slowly, bringing more new stars into

*Grand Central Station: the main railway station in New York.

view, and then a great red sun appeared in the window. It was many times larger than the Moon as seen from Earth. Bowman could look at it without discomfort; judging by its colour, it was not hotter than a dying coal. This was a star that had left behind the fire of its youth, and was settling into a peaceful middle age.

The vehicle stopped turning; the great sun lay straight in front. Though there was no feeling of movement, Bowman could tell that he was getting closer to it. Ahead of him, one of the stars was becoming rapidly brighter, and was beginning to move against its background. It came up to him with unexpected speed; and he saw that it was not a world at all.

It was an enormous structure of metal, hundreds of kilometres across. In different places across its surface were great buildings which were as large as cities, and arranged around these, in neat rows and lines, were hundreds of smaller objects. After some time Bowman realized that these were spaceships. He was flying over an enormous orbital car park.

Because he could see no familiar object, it was almost impossible to calculate the size of the ships. But some were certainly enormous; perhaps kilometres long. They were of many different designs – round balls, thin pencils, flat circles. This must be one of the meeting places for the commercial traffic of the stars.

Or it had been – perhaps a million years ago. Bowman could not see any signs of activity anywhere. This great space-port was as dead as the Moon.

It was not only the absence of movement. There were great holes in the structure, caused by asteroids crashing through it over many years. This was not a working car-park now; it was a resting place for dead vehicles.

He had missed its builders by ages, and when he understood this, Bowman's heart sank. He had not known what to expect, but at least he had hoped to meet with some intelligence. Now, it seemed, he was too late. He had been caught in an ancient, automatic trap, which was still working when its makers had died long ago. It had carried him across the Galaxy, and left him in this dead sea of stars to die when his air-supply ended.

Well, he had already seen wonderful things for which many men would give their lives. Four of his companions already had; he had no reason to complain.

The ruined space-port was still sliding past him at high speed. In a few more minutes, it had fallen behind.

His destination was not there − but far ahead in the great red sun which his vehicle was unmistakably falling towards.

Chapter 43   Fireball

Now there was only the red sun filling the sky from side to side. He was so close now that he could see great clouds of gas moving across its surface.

He did not even try to understand how big this planet was. The sizes of Jupiter and Saturn had been beyond his imagination, but everything here was a hundred times larger. He could only accept the pictures that were flooding into his mind, without attempting to think what they meant.

As that sea of fire grew beneath him, Bowman expected to be afraid − but, curiously, he now felt only a slight nervousness. He knew that he was under the protection of a higher intelligence. He was now very close to the red sun, but someone − or something − was protecting him from the heat, so perhaps there was reason to hope.

The vehicle was now moving in a shallow curve almost parallel to the surface of the star. And, as he looked down, Bowman saw something new. Moving across the ocean of hot gas were thousands of bright spots. They shone in a soft light that became brighter and fainter every few seconds. And they were all travelling in the same direction, like fish moving up a river. Bowman felt that their movement had some purpose. He would probably never know what it was.

He was moving through a new kind of world, which few people had ever dreamed of. Beyond sea and land and air and space lay the regions of fire, which only he had been lucky enough to see. It was too much to expect that he would also understand.

Chapter 44   Reception

It seemed that walls of some material like smoked glass were thickening around him, cutting out the red light and hiding the view. It became darker and darker. A moment later, the vehicle settled on a hard surface and stopped.

Stopped on *what*? Bowman asked himself. Then light returned and, as he looked around him, Bowman knew he must be mad. He was prepared, he thought, for anything. But he had never expected everything to be completely ordinary.

The vehicle was resting on the polished floor of a large hotel room, the same kind of room that you might find in any city on Earth. He was staring at a coffee table, a sofa, a dozen chairs, a writing desk, various lamps, a half-filled bookcase with some magazines lying on it, and even a bowl of flowers.

For many minutes Bowman did not move from his seat. It all seemed real, but there was still the question of air. So he closed the helmet of his suit. Then he opened the door of the vehicle and stepped out into the room.

Like a man in a dream, he walked across to the coffee table. On it sat a normal Bell System Picturephone, complete with local phone book. He bent down and picked it up with his thick gloved hands.

It showed, in the familiar type he had seen thousands of times, the name: *WASHINGTON DC*. Then he looked more closely and, for the first time, he had proof that, although all this might look real, he was not on Earth.

He could read only the word *WASHINGTON*; the rest of the printing was unclear, like a copy of a newspaper photograph. He opened the book and looked through the pages. They were all plain sheets of white material which certainly was not paper, though it looked very much like it.

He lifted the telephone and pressed it against the plastic of his helmet. If there had been any sound, he would have heard it. But, as he had expected, there was only silence.

So – it was all a copy, though a very careful one. And it was clearly not intended to deceive but – he hoped – to make him feel at home. He would not remove his suit, though, until he had completed his voyage of exploration.

There were two doors that opened easily. The first one took him into a small but comfortable bedroom. He opened a cupboard door and found four suits, white shirts, underwear and pyjamas.

Next to the bedroom was a bathroom with all the expected things, all of which worked in a perfectly normal manner. And after that was a small kitchen with electric cooker, fridge, cupboards and drawers, sink, table and chairs. Bowman realized that he was hungry.

First he opened the fridge. The shelves were filled with packages and cans; they all looked perfectly familiar from a distance, though the print on their labels was unclear. However, there were no eggs, milk, butter, fruit, or any other types of unprocessed food.

Bowman picked up a package. The larger words on it said that it contained bread, but it seemed too heavy. He opened the paper at one end. It was full of a blue substance. Apart from its odd colour, it looked rather like bread pudding.

But this is silly, Bowman told himself. I am almost certainly being watched, and I must look a fool wearing this suit. If this is an intelligence test, I've probably failed already.

Without hesitation, he walked back into the bedroom and began to undo his helmet. When it was loose, he lifted it a little and smelled the atmosphere cautiously. He seemed to be breathing perfectly normal air.

He dropped the helmet on the bed and took off his suit. Then he walked back into the kitchen and ate some of the blue substance. The taste was complicated, but pleasant enough. He looked around for something to drink. There were some cans of beer at the back of the fridge. He opened one, and found that it held more of the blue food.

In a few seconds, he had opened half a dozen of the other packages and cans. Whatever their labels, their contents were the same. So he filled a glass with water from the kitchen tap, and tasted it cautiously.

It was terrible, but that was because it had no taste at all; the tap was supplying totally pure water. His hosts were obviously taking no chances with his health.

Feeling much better, he then had a quick shower and dressed himself in clothes from the cupboard. He lay down on the bed. Above it was the usual hotel-type ceiling TV screen. At first he thought that, like the telephone, it was just a copy. But the control unit beside the bed looked so real that his fingers moved to the ON button. The screen lit up.

He pressed the channel button, and saw a well-known African broadcaster, discussing his country's wild life. Bowman listened for a few seconds, happy to hear a human voice again. Then he changed channels and found himself watching a cowboy film. He changed again and again, and saw a number of TV programmes from different parts of the world.

However, all of them were about two years old. That was

around the time TMA-1 had been discovered. It meant that the black object had spent its time recording the radio waves.

He continued to change channels, and suddenly recognized a familiar scene. There, on the screen, was the room he had first arrived in. However, instead of his vehicle, it contained a famous actor who was having a noisy argument with an actress. Bowman was shocked at first – and when the camera followed the angry couple to the bedroom, he almost expected someone to come in.

So his hosts had based their idea of life on Earth on TV programmes. He had learned all he needed to know for the moment, so he turned off the set. He knew he was exhausted, but it seemed impossible that he could sleep. He switched off the light, and within seconds had passed beyond the reach of dreams.

For the last time, David Bowman slept.

Chapter 45   Memories

Since there was no more use for them, the hotel rooms disappeared back into the mind of their creator. Only the bed remained, on which David Bowman lay. He did not wake; he did not dream. Something entered his mind, and he moved into a type of consciousness that no man had ever experienced before. At first it seemed that Time was running backwards, but then he understood.

His memory was being examined. He was reliving his past, one experience at a time. There was the living-room with its coffee table and telephone – there the vehicle – there the burning red sun – there the black hole he had fallen so far down.

Now he was on *Discovery* again, and the rings of Saturn filled the sky. Before that he was talking to Hal, talking to Frank Poole, talking to Earth.

He was travelling back down the passages of time. All his

knowledge and experience was leaving him as he moved back to his childhood. But nothing was being lost; everything that he had ever been, at every moment of his life, was being moved to a safer place. As one David Bowman died, another would continue to live.

And in an empty room, in the fires of a star twenty-thousand light years from Earth, a baby opened its eyes and began to cry.

Chapter 46   Star-Child

Then it became silent, as it saw that it was not alone.

A ghostly, shining square had formed in the empty air. Moving across it were bars of light and shadow.

It was a sight to hold the attention of any child – or any man-ape. But, as it had been three million years before, it was only the outside shape of more complicated forces. It held the baby's attention, while his mind was examined and explored, and changed.

With eyes that already held more than human intelligence, the baby stared at the glass object, seeing – but not yet understanding – the mysteries that lay beyond. It knew that it had come home, that here was the beginning of many races besides its own, but it also knew that it could not stay. Beyond this lay another birth, stranger than any in the past, and now the moment had come.

The metal and plastic of the forgotten vehicle, and the clothing once worn by David Bowman, flashed into flame. The last connections with Earth were gone.

But the child hardly noticed. He knew that he was still a baby, and would remain one until he had decided on a new form. Or he might pass beyond the need for any form.

And now it was time to go. He knew his destination, but there was no need to return the way he had come. With three million years of knowledge, he now understood that there were more ways than one to move through space. The ancient Star Gate had served him well, but he would not need it again.

Confident, because he knew that he was not alone, he travelled across the light-years. Stars slipped past on each side at unbelievable speed. The Milky Way became faint as it fell behind him.

Then he was back, exactly where he wished to be, in the space that men called real.

There before him, a shining toy that no Star-Child could ignore, floated the planet Earth with all its peoples.

He had returned in time. Down there the alarms would be flashing across computer screens as the human race prepared for its final war.

A thousand kilometres below, he saw that a bomb was going to explode in the atmosphere. It was no danger to him, but he preferred a cleaner sky. He held it in his mind, and it burned quickly and silently.

Then he waited, wondering about his other untested powers. Though he was master of the world, he was not quite sure what to do next.

But he would think of something.

ACTIVITIES

PART ONE

Before you read

1 The science fiction book *2001: A Space Odyssey* came out in 1968. What was happening in space travel at the time? What might Arthur C. Clarke imagine would happen by the year 2001?

2 Match these words with the definitions below. The words are all in the story.

   ape   leopard   odyssey   slope   steward   structure

   a the side of a hill or valley
   b a person who looks after passengers on a plane
   c a long, interesting journey
   d an animal like a monkey, but larger and without a tail
   e an object or form with connected parts
   f a large yellow cat with black spots

After you read

3 Who or what:
   a is nearly a metre and a half high, though very thin?
   b are the only animals who look up at the moon?
   c gives commands that lead to the development of Man?
   d is killed by new weapons?

4 The sentences below describe steps in the development of human beings. Each change – except the first – happened because of one of the others. Put the sentences in order.
   a They could make more sounds.
   b Their teeth became smaller.
   c They could pass on knowledge.
   d They could cut meat up with stones.
   e Speech became possible.
   f Their jaws became shorter.

PART TWO

Before you read

5 Discuss the final sentence of PART ONE: 'But now, as long as they existed, he was living on borrowed time.'

    a Who are ' they' and 'he'?

    b What does the writer mean by this sentence?

6 Find these words in your dictionary. Discuss why each word might be useful for talking about space travel.

    airlock   anomaly   astronaut   crater   experiment   gravity
    helmet   horizon   (loud)speaker   magnetic   orbit   reflect

After you read

7 Who asks these questions? What are the true answers?

    a 'Is it really true about illness on the Moon?'

    b 'Do you know what TMA-1 means?'

    c 'Would you like to go to Earth?'

8 Look at this page from Floyd's notebook:

Where did TMA-1 come from?

The Moon?   One of the planets?   The stars?

Each of these possibilities has problems. Discuss them with another student, and try to find a solution.

PART THREE

Before you read

9 'A pattern of energy had jumped from the face of the Moon and was heading out towards the stars.' What might this energy be? How might it affect people on Earth and in space?

10 Find a connection between a word in *italics* and a pair of words below.

asteroid   hibernate   mission   probe   satellite   telescope

a journey, job
b far, see
c cold, sleep
d rock, space
e spaceship, unmanned
f space, circling

After you read

11 Are these sentences true or false?
a Mars is nearer Earth than Jupiter is.
b Saturn is sixty times the size of Earth.
c Many asteroids are more than one hundred kilometres across.
d Saturn has more moons than Jupiter.

12 Describe everyday life on *Discovery* for the five human members of the crew.

PART FOUR

Before you read

13 This part begins with Poole's family, on Earth, wishing him a happy birthday. What might they say? What do you think they are all thinking?

14 Check the meanings of the words in *italics* in your dictionary. Then use these words to complete the definitions of the words:

air   equipment   gas   machine   moon   radio   TV

a *antenna* It is fixed outside and receives ..... .
or ..... signals.
b *lunar* Connected with the ..... .
c *unit* A small piece of ..... which is part of
a larger ..... .
d *vacuum* A space where there is no ..... or any
other ..... .

15 Discuss why the AE 35 unit is important to the development of the story.

16 If Bowman meets with life on Japetus, he may want to report on human progress since TMA-1 was left on the Moon. Work with another student and make a list of the best and worst things that people have done.

PARTS FIVE AND SIX

Before you read

17 The next chapter is called 'Survival'. What do you think Bowman's problems will be? Which ones can he solve?

18 What are the words in *italics* in your language?

    a A *galaxy* is an enormous group of stars, billions of kilometres across.

    b Things with the shape of an egg or an eye or a human face are *oval*.

After you read

19 On the last page of the story, the Star-Child prevents a bomb from exploding, and is not quite sure what to do next. What would *you* do to improve the world? Discuss your ideas with another student.

Writing

20 The writer suggests that human progress began when early man-apes learned how to use weapons and to kill. Many people would disagree. Write your own views on this subject.

21 Bowman knows that he will never return to Earth. Imagine that he writes about the things he remembers best, and what he misses most. Write down his ideas.

22 After the rest of the crew die, you are asked by Mission Control to talk to Bowman about the problems of loneliness. Write down what you will say to him.

23 After TMA-1 is discovered, a meeting is held in Washington to decide whether to tell the people of the world about intelligent life in space. You have been asked to give your views. Write your speech.

24 This book appeared in 1968. How accurate were Arthur C. Clarke's ideas about life in the year 2001?

25 *2001: A Space Odyssey* is also a great film. If you have seen the film, compare the ways in which the film and the book affected you. Which did you prefer? Why? If you have not seen the film, choose a scene from the book and explain how it could best be filmed now.

BESTSELLING
PENGUIN READERS

AT LEVEL 5

The Body

The Firm

Four Weddings and a Funeral

The Great Gatsby

Jane Eyre

The Pelican Brief

The Prisoner of Zenda

Rebecca

Tales from Shakespeare

Taste and Other Tales

A Time to Kill

Wuthering Heights

THE BEST WEBSITES FOR STUDENTS OF ENGLISH!

www.penguinreaders.com

Where the world of Penguin Readers comes to life

- Fully searchable on-line catalogue
- Downloadable resource materials
- First ever on-line Penguin Reader!
- New competition each month!

www.penguindossiers.com

Up-to-the-minute website providing articles for free!

- Articles about your favourite stars, blockbuster movies and big sports events!
- Written in simple English with fun activities!

NEW from Penguin Readers
Your favourite titles on Audio CD

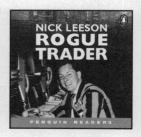